# LIVES OF THE HUNTED

Containing a True Account of the DOINGS
of *Five* QUADRUPEDS & *Three* BIRDS,
and, in *Elucidation* of the Same,
over **200** DRAWINGS ♪♪♪

AUTHOR OF *Wild Animals I have Known*, Trail of the *Sandhill Stag*, BIOGRAPHY
of a *Grizzly*, etcetera & NATURALIST *to the* GOVERNMENT
of **MANITOBA**.

Published by HODDER & STOUGHTON, LIMITED

British Library Cataloguing-in-Publication Data
A catalogue record for this book is available from the
British Library

# Ernest Thompson Seton

Ernest Thompson Seton was born on 14th August 1860, in South Shields, County Durham, England. He grew up to be a pioneering author, wildlife artist, founder of the Woodcraft Indians, and one of the originators of the Boy Scouts of America (BSA).

The Seton family emigrated to Canada when Ernest was just six years old, and most of his childhood was consequently spent in Toronto. As a youth, he retreated to the woods to draw and study animals as a way of avoiding his abusive father – a practice which shaped the rest of his adult life. On his twenty-first birthday, Seton's father presented him with a bill for all the expenses connected with his childhood and youth, including the fee charged by the doctor who delivered him. He paid the bill, but never spoke to his father again.

Originally known as Ernest Evan Thompson, Ernest changed his name to Ernest Thompson Seton, believing that Seton had been an important name in his paternal line. He became successful as a writer, artist and naturalist, and moved to New York City to further his career. Seton later lived at 'Wyndygoul', an estate that he built in Cos Cob, a section of Greenwich, Connecticut. After experiencing vandalism by some local youths, Seton invited the young miscreants to his estate for a weekend, where he told them what he claimed were stories of the American Indians and of nature.

After this experience, he formed the Woodcraft Indians (an American youth programme) in 1902 and invited the local youth to join (at first just boys, but later girls as well). The stories that Seton told became a series of articles written for the *Ladies Home Journal*, and were eventually collected in *The Birch Bark Roll of the Woodcraft Indians* in 1906. Seton also met Scouting's founder, Lord Baden-Powell, in 1906. Baden-Powell had read Seton's book of stories, and was greatly intrigued by it. After the pair had met and shared ideas, Baden-Powell went on to found the Scouting movement worldwide, and Seton became vital in the foundation of the Boy Scouts of America (BSA) and was its first Chief Scout (from 1910 – 1915). Despite this large achievement, Seton quickly became embroiled in disputes with the BSA's other founders, Daniel Carter Beard and James E. West.

In addition to disputes about the content of Seton's contributions to the Boy Scout Handbook, conflicts also arose about the suffrage activities of his wife, Grace, and his British citizenship (it being *an American* organization). In his personal life, Seton was married twice. The first time was to Grace Gallatin in 1896, with whom he had one daughter, Ann (who later changed her name to Anya), and secondly to Julia M. Buttree, with whom he adopted an infant daughter, Beulah (who also changed her first name, to Dee). Alongside his work with the Woodcraft Indians and the BSA, Seton also found time to pursue his primary interest – that of nature writing.

Seton was an early pioneer of animal fiction writing, his most popular work being *Wild Animals I Have Known* (1898), which contains the story of his killing of the wolf Lobo. He later became involved in a literary debate known as the nature fakers controversy, after John Burroughs published an article in 1903 in the *Atlantic Monthly* attacking writers of sentimental animal stories. The controversy lasted for four years and included important

American environmental and political figures of the day, including President Theodore Roosevelt. Seton was also associated with the Santa Fe arts and literary community during the mid-1930s and early 1940s, which comprised a group of artists and authors including author and artist Alfred Morang, sculptor and potter Clem Hull, painter Georgia O'Keeffe, painter Randall Davey, painter Raymond Jonson, leader of the Transcendental Painters Group, and artist Eliseo Rodriguez.

In 1931, Seton became a United States citizen. He died on 23rd October, 1946 (aged eighty-six) in Seton Village in northern New Mexico. Seton was cremated in Albuquerque. In 1960, in honour of his 100th birthday and the 350th anniversary of Santa Fe, his daughter Dee and his grandson, Seton Cottier (son of Anya), in a fitting tribute to the man who loved his surrounding countryside so much, scattered his ashes over Seton Village from an airplane.

To the
## Preservation of Our Wild Creatures
### I dedicate this Book

E. S.

# A List of the Stories in this Book

## And their Full-page Drawings

# A List of the Stories in this Book

## A List of the Stories in this Book

# Note to the Reader

In offering this volume of Animal Stories, I might properly repeat much of the Introduction to " Wild Animals I have Known."

In my previous books I have tried to emphasize our kinship with the animals by showing that in them we can find the virtues most admired in Man. Lobo stands for Dignity and Love-constancy; Silverspot, for Sagacity; Redruff, for Obedience; Bingo, for Fidelity; Vixen and Molly Cottontail, for Mother-love; Wahb, for Physical Force; and the Pacing Mustang, for the Love of Liberty. In this volume, Majesty, Grace, the Power of Wisdom, the sweet Uses of Adversity, and the two-edged Sorrows of Rebellion are similarly set forth.

The material of the accounts is true. The chief liberty taken, is in ascribing to one animal the adventures of several.

Of course we know nothing of the lamb-days of Krag. I have constructed them out of frag-

## Note to the Reader

ments from the lives of many mountain-lambs. But the latter parts, the long hunt and the death of Scotty MacDougall, are purely historical. The picture of the horns is photographically correct. They now hang, I believe, in the home of an English nobleman.

"Tito" is very composite. The greyhound incident in which Tito lost her tail was related to me by Major John H. Calef, U. S. A. The other circumstances are chiefly from my own observation.

"Johnny" is almost without deviation from the facts.

The "Kangaroo Rat" is compounded of two, and the "Troubadour" of several, individuals.

"Chink" is entirely true.

The "Chickadee" is, of course, true only in its underlying facts. This is one of a series of stories written in the period from 1881 to 1893, and published in various magazines. It is inserted as an example of my early work, when I used the archaic method, making the animals talk. "Molly Cottontail" was one of this series. It was written in 1888, and in part published in

# Note to the Reader

"St. Nicholas," October, 1890. Since then I have adhered to the more scientific method, of which "Lobo" is my earliest important example. This was written in February, 1894, for "Scribner's Magazine," and published November, 1894.

For the wild animal there is no such thing as a gentle decline in peaceful old age. Its life is spent at the front, in line of battle, and as soon as its powers begin to wane in the least, its enemies become too strong for it; it falls.

There is only one way to make an animal's history un-tragic, and that is to stop before the last chapter. This I have done in "Tito," the "Teal," and the "Kangaroo Rat."

The public has not fully understood the part that Grace Gallatin Seton-Thompson does in my work. The stories are written by myself, and all the pictures, including the marginals, are my own handiwork; but in choice of subject to illustrate, in ideas of its treatment, in the technical book-making, and the preliminary designs for cover and title-page, and in the literary revision of the text, her assistance has been essential.

In giving special credit for the book-making,

## Note to the Reader

I am standing for a principle. Give a person credit for his work, and he will put his heart in it. Every book lovingly made should bear the maker's name; then we should have more books of the kind that the old masters left behind.

I have been bitterly denounced, first, for killing Lobo; second, and chiefly, for telling of it, to the distress of many tender hearts.

To this I reply: In what frame of mind are my hearers left with regard to the animal? Are their sympathies quickened toward the man who killed him, or toward the noble creature who, superior to every trial, died as he had lived, dignified, fearless, and steadfast?

In answer to a question many times put, I may say that I do not champion any theory of diet. I do not intend primarily to denounce certain field sports, or even cruelty to animals. My chief motive, my most earnest underlying wish, has been to stop the extermination of harmless wild animals; not for their sakes, but for ours, firmly believing that each of our native wild creatures is in itself a precious heritage that we have no right to destroy or put beyond the reach of our children.

## Note to the Reader

I have tried to stop the stupid and brutal work of destruction by an appeal—not to reason: that has failed hitherto—but to sympathy, and especially the sympathies of the coming generation.

Men spend millions of dollars each year on pictures. Why not? It is money well spent; good pictures give lasting and elevating pleasure to all who see them. At the same time men spend much labor and ingenuity in destroying harmless wild animals. No good, but great mischief, comes of this extermination. The main reason for preserving good pictures applies to the preservation of most animals. There will always be wild land not required for settlement; and how can we better use it than by making it a sanctuary for living Wild Things that afford pure pleasure to all who see them?

E. S.

# Krag, the Kootenay Ram

# Krag, the Kootenay Ram

A GREAT broad web of satin, shining white, and, strewn across, long clumps and trailing wreaths of li- lac, almost white, wistaria bloom,—pendent, shining, and so delicately wrought in palest silk that still the web was white; and in and out and trailed across, now lost, now plain, two slender, twining, intertwining chains of golden thread.

## I

I SEE a broken upland in the far Northwest. Its gray and purple rocks are interpatched with colors rich and warm, the new-born colors of the upland spring, the greatest springtime in the world; for where there is no winter there can be no spring. The gloom is measure of

17

the light. So, in this land of long, long winter night, where Nature stints her joys for six hard months, then owns her debt and pays it all at once, the spring is glorious compensation for the past. Six months' arrears of joy are paid in one vast lavish outpour. And latest May is made the date of payment. Then spring, great, gorgeous, sixfold spring, holds carnival on every ridge.

Even the sullen Gunder Peak, that pierces the north end of the ridge, unsombres just a whit. The upland beams with all the flowers it might have grown in six lost months; yet we see only one. Here by our feet, and farther on, and right and left and onward far away, in great, broad acre beds, the purple lupine blooming. Irregular, broken, straggling patches near, but broader, denser, farther on; till on the distant slopes they lie, long, devious belts, like purple clouds at rest.

But late May though it be, the wind is cold; the pools tell yet of frost at night. The White Wind blows. Broad clouds come up, and down comes driving snow, over the peaks, over the upland, and over the upland flowers. Hoary,

18

gray, and white the landscape grows in turn;
and one by one the flowers are painted out.
But the lupines, on their taller, stiffer stems, can
fight the snow for long : they bow their whitened
heads beneath its load; then, thanks no little
to the wind itself, shake free and stand up
defiantly straight, as fits their royal purple.
And when the snowfall ends as suddenly as it
began, the clouds roll by, and the blue sky sees
an upland shining white, but streaked and
patched with blots and belts of lovely purple
bloom.

And wound across, and in and out, are two
long trails of track.

## II

LATE snow is good trailing, and Scotty Mac-
Dougall took down his rifle and climbed the
open hills behind his shanty on Tobacco Creek,
toward the well-known Mountain Sheep range.
The broad white upland, with its lupine bands
and patches, had no claim on Scotty's notice,
nor was his interest aroused until he came on
the double trail in the new snow.   At a glance
he read it—two full-grown female Mountain

# Krag, the Kootenay Ram

Sheep wandering here and there across the country, with their noses to the wind. Scotty followed the prints for a short time, and learned that the Sheep were uneasy, but not alarmed, and less than an hour ahead. They had wandered from one sheltered place to another; once or twice had lain down for a minute, only to rise and move on, apparently not hungry, as the abundant food was untouched.

Scotty pushed forward cautiously, scanning the distance, and keeping watch on the trail without following it, when, all at once, he swung around a rocky point into view of a little lupine-crowded hollow, and from the middle of it leaped the two Sheep.

Up went his rifle, and in a moment one or both would have fallen, had not Scotty's eye, before he pulled, rested on two tiny new-born Lambs, that got up on their long, wabbly legs, in doubt, for a moment, whether to go to the newcomer or to follow their mothers.

The old Sheep bleated a shrill alarm to their young, and circled back. The Lambs' moment of indecision was over; they felt that their duty lay with the creatures that looked and smelled like themselves, and coolly turned their uncertain steps to follow their mothers.

Of course Scotty could have shot any or all of the Sheep, as he was within twenty yards of the farthest ; but there is in man an unreasoning impulse, a wild hankering to "catch alive" ; and without thinking of what he could do with them afterward, Scotty, seeing them so easily in his power, leaned his gun in a safe place and ran after the Lambs. But the distressed mothers had by now communicated a good deal of their alarm to their young ; the little things were no longer in doubt that they should avoid the stranger ; and when he rushed forward, his onset added the necessary final touch, and for the first time in their brief lives they knew danger, and instinctively sought to escape it. They were not yet an hour old, but Nature had equipped them with a set of valuable instincts. And though the Lambs were slow of foot compared with the man, they showed at once a singular aptitude at dodging, and Scotty failed to secure them—as he had expected.

Meanwhile the mothers circled about, bleating piteously and urging the little ones to escape.

# Krag, the Kootenay Ram

Scotty, plunging around in his attempt, alarmed them more and more, and they put forth all the strength of their feeble limbs in the effort to go to their mothers. The man slipping and scrambling after them was unable to catch either, although more than once he touched one with his hand. But very soon this serious game of tag was adroitly steered by the timid mothers away from the lupine bed, and once on the smooth, firmer ground, the Lambs got an advantage that quite offset the weariness they began to feel; and Scotty, plunging and chasing first this way and then that, did not realize that the whole thing was being managed by the old ones, till they reached the lowest spur of the Gunder Peak, a ragged, broken, rocky cliff, up which the mothers bounded. Then the little ones felt a new power, just as a young Duck must when first he drops in the water. Their little black rubber hoofs gripped the slippery rocks as no man's foot can do it, and they soared on their new-found mountain wings, up and away, till led by their mothers out of sight.

It was well for them that Scotty had laid aside his rifle, for a Sheep at a hundred yards was as good as dead when he pulled on it. He now rushed back for his weapon, but before he could harm them, a bank of fog from the Peak came rolling between. The same White Wind that brought the treacherous trailing snow that had betrayed them to their deadliest foe, now brought the fog that screened them from his view.

So Scotty could only stare up the cliff and, half in admiration, mutter: "The little divils the little divils—too smart for me, and them less'n an hour old."

For now he fully knew the meaning of the uneasy wandering that he had read in the old ones' trails.

He spent the rest of the day in bootless hunting, and at night went home hungry, to dine off a lump of fat bacon.


### III

THE rugged peaks are not the chosen home, but rather the safe and final refuge, of the Sheep. Once there, the mothers felt no fear, and thenceforth, in the weeks that followed, they took care that in feeding they should never wander far on the open away from their haven on the crags.

The Lambs were of a sturdy stock, and grew so fast that within a week they were strong enough to keep up with their mothers when the sudden appearance of a Mountain Lion forced them all to run for their lives.

The snow of the Lambs' birthday had gone again within a few hours, and all the hills were now carpeted with grass and flowers. The abundant food for the mothers meant plenty of the best for the young ones, and they waggled their tails in satisfaction as they helped themselves.

One of the Lambs, whose distinguishing mark was a very white nose, was stockily built, while his playmate, slightly taller and more graceful, was peculiar in having little nubbins of horns within a few days of his birth.

They were fairly matched, and frisked and raced alongside their mothers or fought together the livelong day. One would dash away, and the other behind him try to butt him; or if they came to an inviting hillock they began at once the world-old, world-wide game of King of the Castle. One would mount and hold his friend

The World-wide Game of King of the Castle.

at bay. Stamping and shaking his little round head, he would give the other to understand that *he* was King of the Castle; and then back would go their pretty pink ears, the round woolly heads would press together, and the innocent brown eyes roll as they tried to look terribly fierce and push and strive, till one, forced to his knees, would wheel and kick up his heels as though to say: "I didn't want your old castle, anyway," but would straightway give himself the lie by seeking out a hillock for himself, and, posing on its top with his fiercest look, would stamp and shake his head, after the way that, in their language, stands for the rhyming challenge in ours, and the combat scene would be repeated.

In these encounters Whitenose generally had the best of it because of his greater weight; but in the races Nubbins was easily first. His activity was tireless; from morning till evening he seemed able to caper and jump.

At night they usually slept close against their mothers, in some sheltered nook where they could see the sunrise, or rather where they could feel it, for that was more important; and Nub-

# Krag, the Kootenay Ram

bins, always active, was sure to be up first of the Lambs. Whitenose was inclined to be lazy, and would stay curled up, the last of the family to begin the day of activity. His snowy nose was matched by a white patch behind, as in all Bighorn Sheep, only larger and whiter than usual, and this patch afforded so tempting a mark that Nubbins never could resist a good chance to charge at it. He was delighted if, in the morning, he could waken his little friend by what he considered a tremendous butt on his beautiful patch of white.

Mountain Sheep usually go in bands; the more in the band, the more eyes for danger. But the hunters had been very active in the Kootenay country; Scotty in particular had been relentless. His shanty roof was littered over with horns of choice Rams, and inside it was half-filled with a great pile of Sheepskins awaiting a market. So the droves of Bighorn were reduced to a few scattering bands, the largest of which was less than thirty, and many, like that of which I speak, had but three or four in it.

Once or twice during the first fortnight of

## Krag, the Kootenay Ram

June old Scotty had crossed the Sheep range, with his rifle ready, for game was always in season for him; but each time, one or the other of the alert mothers saw him afar, and either led quickly away, or, by giving a short, peculiar *sniff*, had warned the others not to move; then all stood still as stones, and so escaped, when a single move might easily have brought sure death. When the enemy was out of sight they quickly changed to some distant part of the range.

But one day, as they rounded a corner of the pine woods, they smelled an unknown smell. They stopped to know what it was, when a large dark animal sprang from a rock and struck Whitenose's mother down.

Nubbins and his mother fled in terror, and the Wolverine, for that was the enemy, put a quick end to her life; but before he began to feast he sprang on Whitenose, who was standing stupefied, and with merciful mercilessness laid him by his mother.

### IV

NUBBINS's mother was a medium-sized, well-knit creature. She had horns longer and sharper

29

than usual for a Ewe, and they were of the kind called Spikehorns or Spikers; she also had plenty of good Sheep sense. The region above Tobacco Creek had been growing more dangerous each month, thanks chiefly to Scotty, and the Mother Sheep's intention to move out was decided for her by the morning's tragedy.

She careered along the slope of the Gunder Peak at full speed, but before going over each rising ground she stopped and looked over it, ahead and back, remaining still as a lichen-patched rock for a minute or more in each place while she scanned the range around.

Once as she did this she saw a dark, moving figure on a range behind her. It was old Scotty. She was in plain view, but she held as still as could be, and so escaped notice; and when the man was lost behind the rocks she bounded away faster than before, with little Nubbins scampering after. At each ridge she looked out carefully; but seeing no more of either her enemy or her friends, she pushed on quietly all that day, travelling more slowly as the danger-field was left behind.

Toward evening, as she mounted the Yak-in-i-

kak watershed, she caught a glimpse of moving forms on a ridge ahead. After a long watch she made out that they were in the uniform of Sheep—gray, with white-striped stockings and white patches on face and stern. They were going up wind. Keeping out of view, she made so as to cross their back trail, which she soon found, and thus learned that her guess was right: there were the tracks of two large Bighorn; but the trail also said that they were Rams. According to Mountain Sheep etiquette, the Rams form one community and the Ewes and Lambs another. They must not mix or seek each other's society, excepting during the early winter, the festal months, the time of love and mating.

Nubbins's mother, or the Spikerdoe, as we may call her, left the trail and went over the watershed, glad to know that this was a Sheep region. She rested for the night in a hollow, and next morning she journeyed on, feeding as she went. Presently the mother caught a scent that made her pause. She followed it a little. Others joined on or crisscrossed, and she knew now that she had found the trail of a band of

31

O

Ewes and Lambs. She followed steadily, and Nubbins skipped alongside, missing his playmate, but making up as far as possible by doing double work.

Within a very few minutes she sighted the band, over a dozen in all—her own people. The top of her head was just over a rock, so that she saw them first; but when Nubbins poked up his round head to see, the slight movement caught the eye of a watchful mother in the flock. She gave the signal that turned all the band to statues, with heads their way. It was now the Spiker's turn. She walked forth in plain view. The band galloped over the hill, but circled behind it to the left, while Nubbins and his mother went to the right.

In this way their positions in the wind were reversed. Formerly she could smell them; now they could smell her; and having already seen her uniform from afar, they were sure her credentials were right. She came cautiously up to them. A leading Ewe walked out to meet her. They sniffed and gazed. The leader stamped her feet, and the Spikerdoe got ready to fight. They advanced; their heads met with

a whack! then, as they pushed, the Spikerdoe
twisted so that one of her sharp points rested
on the other Ewe's ear. The pressure became
very unpleasant. The enemy felt she was getting the worst of it, so she sniffed, turned, and,
shaking her head, rejoined her friends. The
Spikerdoe walked after her, while little Nubbins,
utterly puzzled, stuck close to her side. The
flock wheeled and ran, but circled back, and as
the Spiker stood her ground, they crowded
around her, and she was admitted one of their
number. This was the ceremony, so far as she
was concerned. But Nubbins had to establish
his own footing. There were some seven or
eight Lambs in the flock. Most of them were
older and bigger than he, and, in common with
some other animals, they were ready to persecute the stranger simply because he was strange.

The first taste of this that Nubbins had was
an unexpected "bang!" behind. It had always
seemed very funny to him when he used to give
Whitenose a surprise of this kind, but now there
seemed nothing funny about it; it was simply
annoying. And when he turned to face the
enemy, another one charged from another direc-

tion ; and whichever way he turned, there was a
Lamb ready to butt at him, till poor Nubbins
was driven to take refuge under his mother.
Of course she could protect him, but he could
not stay there always, and the rest of the day
with the herd was an unhappy one for poor
Nubbins, but a very amusing one for the
others. He was so awed by their numbers,
the suddenness of it all, that he did not know
what to do. His activity helped but little.
Next morning it was clear that the others intended to have some more fun at his expense.
One of these, the largest, was a stocky little
Ram. He had no horns yet, but when they
did come they were just like himself, thick-set
and crooked and rough, so that, reading ahead,
we may style him " Krinklehorn." He came
over, and just as Nubbins rose, hind legs first,
as is Sheep fashion, the other hit him square
and hard. Nubbins went sprawling, but jumped
up again, and in something like a little temper
went for the bully. Their small heads came
together with about as much noise as two balls
of yarn, but they both meant to win. Nubbins
was aroused now, and he dashed for that other

34

## Krag, the Kootenay Ram

fellow. Their heads slipped past, and now it
was head to shoulder, both pounding away.
At first Nubbins was being forced back; but
soon his unusual sprouts of horns did good service, and after getting one or two punches in
his ribs from them, the bully turned and ran.
The others, standing round, realized that the
newcomer was fit. They received him as one
of their number, and the hazing of Nubbins was
ended.

### V

It is quite common to hear conventionality
and social rules derided as though they were
silly man-made tyrannies. They are really important laws that, like gravitation, were here
before human society began, and shaped it
when it came. In all wild animals we see them
grown with the mental growth of the species.

When a new Hen or Cow appears in the barn-
yard, she must find her level. She must take
rank exactly according to the sum of her powers.
Those already there have long ago ranged
themselves in a scale of precedence; no one can
climb in this scale without fighting all those

35

# Krag, the Kootenay Ram

over whom she would go.  Somewhere in this
scale there must be a place for the newcomer,
and until this is settled, her life is one of battles.

No doubt strength, courage, and activity fix
her standing in most cases, but sometimes wisdom and keenness of sense are of greater importance.  Which one is the leader of a band
of wild animals?  Not necessarily the strongest
or fiercest.  That one might *drive* the rest, but
not lead them.  The leader is not formally
elected, as with man, but is rather slowly selected, thus, *that individual* who can impress
the rest with the idea that he or she is *the best
one to follow* becomes the leader, and the government is wholly by consent of the governed.
The election is quite unanimous.  For if in
the herd are some who do not care to follow,
they are free to go the other way.  In many
kinds of animals that go in herds, the leader
whose courage and prowess have so often stood
all tests, and who has inspired all the rest with
confidence in his sagacity, is usually not the
strongest male, but an *elderly female*.  This is
especially the case with Elk, Buffalo, Blacktail,
and the summer bands of Mountain Sheep.

36

# Krag, the Kootenay Ram

The Gunder Peak band of Sheep was made up of six or seven Ewes with their Lambs, three or four Yearlings, and a promising young rising Ram, two years of age, and just beginning to be very proud of his horns, now in what is called the " ibex " stage. He was the largest member of the band, but not by any means the most important. The leader was a sagacious old Ewe; not the one that had tried a round with the Spikerdoe, but a smaller one with short, stubby horns, who was none other than the mother of Krinklehorn, the little bully.

The Sheep think of this leader, not as one *to be obeyed*, but as the one *safe to follow*, the one who is always wise; and though they do not give one another names, they have this idea; therefore I shall speak of her as the Wise One.

The Spikerdoe was a very active Sheep, in her early prime, cool, sagacious, keen of eye, nose, and ear, and forever on the watch. At least once in three steps she raised her head to look around, and if she saw anything strange or anything moving, she did not cease gazing until she had made it out and went on grazing again, or else gave the long *snoof* that made

them all stand like stocks. Of course she was only doing what they all did, but happened to do it better than they. The Wise One, however, was rarely far behind her, and sometimes ahead in seeing things, and had the advantage of knowing the country; but they were so nearly matched in gifts that very soon the Wise One felt that in the Spikerdoe she had a dangerous rival for the leadership.

The band was not without its cranks. There was a young Ewe that had a lazy fashion of feeding on her front "knees." The others did not copy her methods: they vaguely felt that they were not good. The effect of this original way of feeding was to bring a great callous pad on each knee (in reality the wrist). Then those growing pads and the improper use of her front legs began to rob Miss Kneepads of her suppleness. She could not spring quickly aside and back as the others could. Ordinarily this does not matter much, but there are times when it is very needful. All animals that must save themselves by flight have developed this trick of zigzag bounding. It is the couching Hare's best foil when sprung at by the Fox or the

Hound; it is the sleeping Rabbit's only counter
to the onset of the Wild Cat; it is the resting
Deer's one balk to the leap of a Wolf; and it
is the plan by which the Snipe, springing zigzag
from the marsh, can set at naught the skill of
the gunner as well as the speed of the Hawk,
until she herself is under full headway.

Another odd Sheep in the band was a nervous little Ewe. She obeyed the leader, except
in one thing. When the short *snoof* turned all
the rest to stone, she would move about, fidget-
ing nervously, instead of heeding the Wise
One's timely order to " freeze."

## VI

SOME weeks went by in frequent alarms and
flights. But the band was ably sentried, and
all went well. As summer drew near a peculiar
feverish restlessness came over the Sheep. They
would stand motionless for a few minutes, neither
grazing nor chewing the cud. They showed
signs of indigestion, and kept on, seeking for
something—they did not know what. As soon
as the Wise One herself felt this listlessness and

loss of appetite, she rose to the occasion. She led the whole band to a lower level, down among the timber, and lower still. Where was she going? The road was new to most of them. The Spikerdoe was full of distrust; she stopped again and again; she did not like these sinister lower levels. But the leader went calmly on. If any of the band had been disposed to stop and go back with her, the Spikerdoe would certainly have made a split. But all went listlessly after the Wise One, whose calm decision really inspired confidence. When far below the safety-line, the leader began to prick up her ears and gaze forward. Those near her also brightened up. They were neither hungry nor thirsty, but their stomachs craved something which they felt was near at last. A wide slope ahead appeared, and down it a white streak. Up to the head of this streak the Wise One led her band. They needed no telling; the bank and all about was white with something that the Sheep eagerly licked up. Oh, it was the most delicious thing they had ever tasted! It seemed they could not get enough; and as they licked and licked, the dryness left their throats, the hotness went

from eye and ear, the headache quit their brains, their fevered itching skins grew cool and their stomachs sweetened, their listlessness was gone, and all their nature toned. It was like a most delicious drink of life-giving cordial, but it was only *common salt*.

This was what they had needed—and this was the great healing Salt-lick to which the leader's wisdom had been their guide.


## VII

FOR a young animal there is no better gift than obedience. It is obedience to the mother that gives him the benefit of all his mother's experience without the risk of getting it. Courage is good; speed and strength are good: but his best courage, speed, and strength are far below those of his mother, and they are at his service to the uttermost, if only he will obey. Brains are all-powerful, but among very young Bighorn Sheep at least, an obedient fool is far better off than the wisest headstrong Lamb that ever drew the breath of life.

When they had lingered an hour or two and

41

licked the salt till nature was satisfied, the Wise
One turned to go back to the range. The
grass in the valley was uncommonly good,
rich, rank, and abundant, and the Lambs
just beginning to feed were revelling in the
choicest of pasture; but this was down among
the timber, with all its furtive dangers. The
Wise One, as well as the Spikerdoe, wanted to
get back to their own safe feeding-ground.
She led the way, and the rest, though unwilling,
would have followed, but little Krinklehorn was
too much engrossed with the rich food. He
would not follow. His mother missed him, and
when he bleated she came back to him. He
did not positively refuse to come, but he lingered so that he held his mother back and encouraged the others to do the same. And when
night fell the band was still below timber-line,
and went to sleep in the woods.

A Mountain Lion does not make much noise
as he sneaks up after his prey; he goes like a
shadow: and not a sound was made by the great
hungry Lion of the Yak-in-i-kak until by chance
one little pebble touched by his velvet foot rolled
down the bank. It was a slight noise, but the

Spikerdoe heard it, and blowing the long *snoooof*, she called little Nubbins, and, in spite of the darkness, dashed up the cliff toward her safe home land. The others also leaped to their feet, but the Lion was among them. The Wise One leaped up, with a sign to Krinklehorn to follow. She also bounded toward safety—was saved; but her Lamb, always wilful, thought he saw a better way of escape, and finding himself alone, he bleated, "*Mother*"; and she, forgetting her own danger, dashed down again, and in a moment the Lion laid her low. Another Sheep forged by, and another, in the hurry and uproar of flight. At each of these in turn the Lion sprang, but each offset his pounce by a succession of bewildering zigzag jumps, and so escaped, till, last of all, poor Kneepads made past for the rocks, and when the Lion leaped she failed to play the only balk. The power that would have saved her she had long ago resigned; so now she fell.

Far up the bench the Sheep went bounding after the one that led. One by one they came up as she slacked her speed, and then they saw that the leader now was Spiker. They never

saw the Wise One again, and so they knew that she must have fallen.

When they had reunited and turned to look back, they heard from far below a faint *baah* of a Lamb.   All cocked their ears and waited. It is not wise to answer too quickly; it may be the trick of some enemy.   But it came again— the familiar *baah* of one of their own flock; and Spikerdoe answered it.

A rattling of stones, a scrambling up banks, another *baah* for guidance, and there appeared among them little Krinklehorn—an orphan now.

Of course he did not know this yet, any more than the others did.   But as the day wore on and no mother came in response to his plaintive calls, and as his little stomach began also to cry out for something more than grass or water, he realized his desolation, and *baahed* more and more plaintively.   When night came he was cold as well as hungry;  he must snuggle up to some one or freeze.   No one took much notice of him, but Spikerdoe, seemingly the new leader, called once or twice in answer to his call, and almost by accident he drifted near her when she

44

Dividing his Birthright.

lay down and warmed himself against her beside his ancient enemy, young Nubbins.

In the morning he seemed to Mother Spiker-doe to be her own, in a limited sense.   Rubbing against Nubbins made him smell like her own. And when Nubbins set about helping himself to a breakfast of warm milk, poor hungry Krinkle-horn took the liberty of joining in on the other side.   Thus Nubbins found himself nose to nose and dividing his birthright with his old-time enemy.   But neither he nor his mother made any objection, and thus it was that Krinklehorn was adopted by his mother's rival.


## VIII

THERE was no one of the others that could equal Spikerdoe in sagacity.   She knew all the range now, and it was soon understood that she was to lead.   It was also understood that Krinklehorn, as well as Nubbins, was her Lamb.   The two were like brothers in many things.   But Krinklehorn had no sense of gratitude to his foster-mother, and he always nursed his old grudge against Nubbins, and

D

## Krag, the Kootenay Ram

now that they drank daily of the same drink,
he viewed Nubbins as his rival, and soon showed
his feeling by a fresh attempt to master him.
But Nubbins was better able to take care
of himself now than ever. Krinklehorn got
nothing but a few good prods for his pains,
and their relative status was settled.

During the rest of the season they grew up
side by side: Krinklehorn thick-set and sulky,
with horns fast growing, but thick and crinkly;
and Nubbins—well! it is not fair to call him
Nubbins any longer, as his horns were growing
fast and long; so that we may henceforth speak
of him as Krag, a name that he got years afterward in the country around Gunder Peak, and
the name by which he went down to history.

During the summer Krag and Krinklehorn
grew in wit as well as in size. They learned all
the ordinary rules of life among Bighorn. They
knew how to give the warning *sniff* when they
saw something, and the danger *snoo-of* when
they were sure it was dangerous. They were
acquainted with all the pathways and could
have gone alone to any of the near salt-licks
when they felt the need of it.

48

# Krag, the Kootenay Ram

They could do the zigzag bounding that
baffles the rush of an enemy, as well as the
stiff-legged jumping which carries them safely
up glassy, slippery slopes. Krag even excelled
his mother in these accomplishments. They
were well equipped to get their own living, they
could eat grass, and so it was time they were
weaned, for Spikerdoe had to lay on her fat to
keep warm in the coming winter. The young-
sters themselves would have been in no hurry
to give up their comforting breakfast, but the
supply began to run short, and the growing
horns of the Lambs began to interfere with the
mother's comfort so much that she proceeded
firmly and finally with their weaning, and long
before the earliest snow flurry grizzled the upland, she had them quite independent of her for
their daily food.

## IX

AMONG the numbers of the band that met their
fate that summer was the two-year-old Ram.
He had no companion of his age and sex, and
his sense of superiority developed a cock-sure-
ness which resulted in his skin being added to

the pile in Scotty's shanty. When the earliest
snows of winter came, all the Lambs were
weaned and doing for themselves, and the Ewes
were fat and flourishing, but, being free from
maternal cares, had thoughts for other matters.
With the early frosts and the bracing air came
the mating season, and, determined to find
their mates, the Sheep travelled about the like-
liest parts of the hills.

Several times during the summer they had
seen one or two great Rams in the distance, but
an exchange of signals had made clear to each
what the other was, and they had avoided each
other's company. But now, when a pair of
large Sheep were sighted, and the usual signals exchanged, there seemed no sign of a
wish to avoid each other. As the two tall
strangers came on, their great size, majestic
forms, and vast curling horns left no doubt
as to their sex, and, proud of their honors and
powers, they pranced forward. But the for-
wardness of Spikerdoe and her band now
gave place to a decided bashfulness. They
turned as though to avoid the newcomers.
This led to pursuit and to much manœuvring

before the two Rams were permitted to join the herd. Then came the inevitable quarrel. The Rams had so far been good friends—were evidently chums; but chumship and love rivalry cannot dwell together. It was the old story— the jealous pang, the seeking for cause, the challenge, and the duel. But these are not always duels to the death. The Rams charged at each other; their horns whacked together till the chips flew from them; but after a few rounds one of them, the lighter, of course, was thrown backward, and, leaping up, he tried to escape. The other followed for a quarter of a mile, and, as he declined a further fight, the victor came proudly back, and claimed and was allowed the position and joys of Sultan of the band.

Krag and Krinklehorn were ignored. They were in awe of the great Ram who now took charge, and they felt that their safest plan was to keep as far as possible away from the present social activities of the flock, as they were not very sure of their own standing.

During the first part of that winter they were under guidance of the Ram. He was a big, handsome fellow, devoted to his female follow-

ing, but not without a streak of masculine self-
ishness that made him take care to have the
best of the food and to keep a sharp lookout
for danger. Food was plentiful, for the Ram
knew enough to lead them not into the sheltered
ravines where the snow was deep, but up on
the bleakest ridges of the upland, where the
frigid wind lays bare the last year's grass, and,
furthermore, where no enemy can approach
unseen; so all went well.

## X

THE springtime came, with its thrilling sounds
and feelings. Obedient to their ancient law,
the Ram and the band of Ewes had parted
company in midwinter. The feeling had been
growing for days. They were less disposed to
follow him, and sometimes he lingered far away
for hours. One day he did not rejoin them,
and thenceforth to the end of the winter they
followed the Spikerdoe as of old.

The little ones came about the first of June.
Many of the mothers had two each, but Spikerdoe, now the Wise One, had but one, as

52

before, and this little one displaced Krag for
good and engrossed all the mother's attention.
He even hindered her in her duties as a leader;
and one day, as she was feeding him and
watching the happy wagging of his tail, another
Sheep gave an alarm. All froze except Fidgets.
She crossed before the Wise One. There
was a far-away "*crack!*" Fidgets dropped
dead, and the Spikerdoe fell with a stifled *baah!*
But she sprang to her feet, forgetting her own
pain, and looking wildly about her for her
Lamb, she leaped on the ridge to follow the
others. Bang! went the rifle again, and the old
Sheep got a first glimpse of the enemy. It was
the man who had once so nearly caught the
Lambs. He was a long way off, but the ball
whistled before the Sheep's nose. She sprang
back and changed her course, thereby leaving
the rest, then leaped over the ridge, bleating to
her little one to follow—bleating, too, from
pain, for she was hard hit. But she leaped
headlong down a rocky place, and the high
ground came between. Down the gully she
bounded, and out along the farther ridge, keeping out of sight so well that, though Scotty ran

as fast as he could to the edge, he never saw
her again. He chuckled as he noted the spots
of blood; but these soon ceased, and after a
long attempt to keep the trail, he gave it up,
cursed his luck, and went back to the victim he
had secured.

Away went Spikerdoe and her Lamb, the
mother guiding, but the little one ahead. Her
instinct told her that upward was the way to
safety. Up the Gunder Peak she must go, but
keep from being seen. So she went on, in spite
of a burning wound, always keeping a ridge between, till round the nearest rocks she paused
to look. She saw no sign either of her friends
or her foe. She felt she had a deadly wound.
She must escape lest her strength give out. She
set off again at a run, forging upward, and the
little one following or running ahead as he
pleased. On they went till the timber-line was
reached, and upward still her instinct urged
her on.

Another lofty bench was scaled, and then
she sighted a long white streak, a snow-drift
lingering in a deep ravine. She eagerly made
for that. There was a burning pain through

54

His Mother . . . . was so Cold and Still.

her loins, and on each side was a dark stain on
her coat.   She craved a cooling touch, and on
reaching the white patch sank on her side, her
wound against the snow.

There could be only one end to such a
wound : two hours, three hours at furthest, and
then — well, never mind.

And the little one?   He stood dumbly gazing at her.   He did not understand.   He only
knew that he was cold and hungry now, and
that his mother, to whom he had looked for
everything, — food, warmth, guidance, and sympathy, — was so cold and still!

He did not understand it.   He did not know
what next.   But we do — the lingering misery,
and the inevitable finish, soon or late, according to his strength ; and the Raven on the rock
knew, and waited.   Better for the Lamb, far
better, quicker, and more merciful, had the
rifle served him as it did his mother.

## XI

KRAG was a fine young Ram now, taller than
any of the Ewes, and with long cimetars of

horns. Krinklehorn also was well grown, as heavy as Krag, but not so tall, and with horns that looked diseased, they were so short, thick, and bumpy.

The autumn came again, with the grand re-union of the families, the readvent of the Ram, and also with a readjustment that Krag had not looked for. He was just beginning to realize that he was a Ram, and to take an interest in certain Ewes in the flock, when the great Ram came, with his curling horns and thick bull neck ; and the first thing he did was to bundle Krag out of the flock. Krag, Krinklehorn, and three or four more of their age were packed off by themselves, for such is etiquette among Sheep. As soon as the young males reach, or nearly reach, maturity they must go off to study life for themselves, just as a boy leaves home for college. And during the four years that followed Krag led a roving bachelor life with a half-dozen companions. He became the leader, for he inherited his mother's wit, and they travelled into far countries, learning new pastures, new ways, and new wisdom, and fitting themselves to become fathers of large and successful

# Krag, the Kootenay Ram

families; for such is the highest ambition of every good Mountain Ram.

It was not choice that left Krag unmated, but a combination of events against which he vainly chafed, and he was still left with his bachelor crew. It was really better so. It seemed hard at the time, but it proved his making, for he was thus enabled to develop to the full his wonderful powers before being hampered and weakened by the responsibilities and mingled joys of a family. Each year the bachelor Rams grew handsomer. Even sulky Krinklehorn became a tall and strong, if not a fine-looking, Ram. He had never gotten over his old dislike of Krag. Once or twice he put forth his strength to worst him, and even tried to put him over a cliff; but he got so severely punished for it that thenceforth he kept away from his foster-brother. But Krag was a joy to behold. As he bounded up the jagged cliffs, barely touching each successive point with his clawed and padded hoofs, floating up like a bird, deriding all foes that thought of following afoot, and the sunbeams changing and flashing from his back as the supple muscles working changed the sur-

59

## Krag, the Kootenay Ram

face form, he was more like a spirit thing, that had no weight and knew no fear of falling, than a great three-hundred-pound Ram with five year-rings on his horns.

And such horns! The bachelors that owned his guidance had various horns, reflecting each the owner's life and gifts: some rough half-moons, some thick, some thin. But Krag's curled in one great sweep, three quarters of a circle, and the five year-marks told, first, begin-ning at the point, of the year when he was a Lamb, and grew the straight long spikes that had helped him so well in his early fight; next year the growth thicker and much longer; the next two years told of yet more robust growth with lesser length; but the last was record of a year of good food, of perfect health, and unexampled growth, for the span grown then was longer, wider, and cleaner horns than any of the others.

Tucked away under the protecting shadow of each rugged base, like things too precious to expose, were his beautiful eyes. Dark brown when he was a Lamb, yellowish brown when a yearling, they were now, in his early prime, great orbs of shining gold, or splendid amber

60

## Krag, the Kootenay Ram

jewels, with a long, dark, misty depth in each, through which the whole bright world was born and mirrored on his brain.

There is no greater joy to the truly living thing than the joy of being alive, of feeling alive in every part and power. It was a joy to Krag now to stretch his perfect limbs in a shock of playful battle with his friends. It was a joy to press his toes on some thin ledge, then sail an impossible distance across some fearful chasm to another ledge, whose size and distance he gauged with absolute precision. It was a joy to him to set the Mountain Lions at naught by a supple ricochet from rock to rock, or to turn and drive the bounding Blacktail band down pell-mell backward to their own, the lower, levels. There was a subtle pleasure in every move, and a glorying in his glorious strength, which, after all, is beauty. And when to such a being the early winter brought also the fire of love and set him all aglow, he was indeed a noble thing to see. In very wantonness of strength and power, he bounded, ball-like, up or down long, rugged slopes, leaping six feet high where one would have fully an-

swered every end except the pleasure of doing
it. But so he went, seeking, searching—for
what? He could not have told; but he
would know when he found it. Away he careered at the head of his band, till they crossed
the trail of another band, and, instinct-guided,
he followed after. In a mile or two the other
band was sighted, a group of Ewes. They fled,
of course, but being cornered on a rugged
bench, they stood, and after due punctilio they
allowed the Rams to approach.

The Bighorn is no monogamist. The finest
Ram claims all of the Ewes in the flock, and
any question of his claim must be settled on
the spot in mortal fight. Hitherto there had
been a spirit of good-fellowship among the
Rams, but now that was changed; and when
great Krag bounded forward, snorting out a
challenge to all the rest to disprove his right of
might, there was none to face him, and, strange
to tell, with many claimants, there was no fight.
There was nothing now for the rest to do but
to wheel at his command and leave him to the
devotion and admiration of his conquest.

If, as they say, beauty and prowess are

winning cards in all walks of animal life, then
Krag must have been the idol of his band. For
matched with Rams he had seemed a wonder,
and among the Ewes his strength, his size, and
the curling horns must have made of him a
demigod, and the winged heart and the brimming cup were his.

But on the second day of joy two Rams appeared, and after manœuvring came near. One
was a fine big animal, as heavy in the body as
Krag, but with smaller horns, and the other
was—yes, it surely was—Krinklehorn. The
new Ram snuffed a challenge as he came near,
then struck the ground with his foot, meaning,
" I am a better Ram than you, and mean to oust
you from your present happy position."

Krag's eyes blazed. He curled his massive
neck. He threw his chin up and down like a
champing horse, shook his great horns as
though they were yet mere points, laid back his
ears, and charged ; and forward sprang the foe.
*Choch!* they came together; but the stranger
had an advantage of ground, which left the first
onset a draw.

The Rams backed off, each measuring the

Ë

other and the distance, and, seeking for firm
footing, kept on the edge of the great bench;
then, with a whoof! they came on again.
Whack! and the splinters flew, for they both
were prime. But this time Krag clearly had
the best of it. He tollowed up his advantage at once with a second whack! at short
range, and twisting around, his left horn hooked
under the right of his foe, when, to his utter
dismay, he received a terrific blow on his flank
from an unknown enemy. He was whirled
around, and would have been dashed over the
cliff but that his horn was locked in that of his
first foe, and so he was saved; for no Ram
has weight enough in his hind quarter to oppose
the headlong charge of another. Krag scrambled
to his feet again, just in time to see the new
enemy irresistibly carried by the violence of his
own charge over the ledge and down.

It was a long time before a far-away crash
told to those on the ledge that Krinklehorn had
found the very end he plotted for his foster-
brother. Ram fights are supposed to be fair
duels. Krinklehorn, failing in fair fight, had
tried foul, and had worked his own destruction;

for not even a Bighorn can drop two hundred feet on rock and live.

Krag now turned on his other foe with double fury. One more shock and the stranger was thrown, defeated. He leaped to his feet and bounded off. For a time Krag urged him to further flight by the same means that Krinkle-horn once used to persecute him, then returned in triumph to live unmolested with his family.

## XII

SCOTTY had gone from his Tobacco Creek location in 1887. The game was pretty well hunted out. Sheep had become very scarce, news of new gold strikes in Colorado had at-tracted him southward, and the old shanty was deserted. Five years went by with Krag as the leading Ram. It was five years under a good genius, with an evil genius removed—five years of prosperity, then, for the Bighorn.

Krag carried further the old ideas that were known to his mother. He taught his band to abjure the lowlands entirely. The forest cov-erts were full of evil, and the only land of safety

# Krag, the Kootenay Ram

was the open, wind-swept peaks, where neither Lions nor riflemen could approach unseen. He found more than one upland salt-lick where their natural need could be supplied without the dangerous lowland journeys that they once had thought necessary. He taught his band never to walk along the top of a ridge, but always along one side, so as to look down both ways without being conspicuous. And he added one famous invention of his own. This was the "hide." If a hunter chances close to a band of Sheep before they see him, the old plan was to make a dash for safety—a good enough plan in the days of bows and arrows or even of muzzle-loading rifles, but the repeating rifle is a different arm. Krag himself learned, and then taught his tribe, to crouch and lie perfectly still when thus surprised. In nine cases out of ten this will baffle a human hunter, as Krag found times without number.

It is always good for a race when a great one arises in it. Krag marked a higher level for the Bighorns. His children multiplied on the Yak-in-i-kak around the Gunder Peak, and eastward as far as Kintla Lake at least. They

66

were healthier and much wiser than had been
the Bighorn of other days, and being so, their
numbers steadily increased.

Five years had made some changes in Krag's
appearance, but his body was square and round
and muscular as ever; his perfect legs seemed
unchanged in form or in force; his head was as
before, with the heart-shaped white patch on
his nose; and his jewel eyes blazed as of old.
But his horns, how they had changed! Before
they were uncommon; now they were unique.
The massive sweeps—the graven records of his
life—were now a circle and a quarter, and they
told of years of joy and years of strife, and one
year, tallied in a narrow band of dark and
wrinkled horn, told of the year when all the
mountains were scourged by the epidemic of
grip—when numbers of Lambs and their mothers died; when many strong Rams suc-
cumbed; when Krag himself had been smitten,
but recovered, thanks to his stalwart growth
and native force, and after a time of misery had
shown no traces of those wretched months,
except in the yearly growth of horn. For that
year, 1889, it was barely an inch in width, plain

for those who read such things—a record of a
time of want.

## XIII

AT length old Scotty came back. Like all
mountaineers, he was a wanderer, and he once
more returned alone to his shanty on Tobacco
Creek. The sod roof had fallen in, and he
hesitated to repair it. Anyhow he would prospect awhile first. He took his rifle and sought
the familiar upland. Before he returned he
had sighted two large bands of Mountain Sheep.
That decided him. He spent a couple of days
repairing the shanty, and the curse of the Yak-
in-i-kak returned.

Scotty was now a middle-aged man. His
hand was strong and steady, but his eyes had
lost some of their power. As a youth he had
scorned all aids to sight; but now he carried a field-glass. In the weeks that followed
he scanned a thousand benches through the
glass, and many a time his eye rested on the
form of the Gunder Ram. The first time he
saw him, he exclaimed, "Heavens, what horns!"
then added prophetically, "Them's mine!"

and he set out to make them his. But the Bighorn of his early days were fools to these, and
month after month passed without his ever
getting a nearer view of the great Ram. The
Ram had more than once seen him at short
range, but Scotty never knew it.

Several times, through the glass, he marked
old Krag from afar on a bench; then, after a
labor of hours, stalked round to the place only
to find him gone. Sometimes he really was
gone, but on more than one occasion the Ram
was close at hand and hidden, watching his foe.

Then came a visitor to Scotty's shanty—a
cattle-man named Lee, a sportsman by instinct,
and a lover of Dogs and Horses. His Horses
were of little use in mountain hunting, but his
Wolf-hounds, three beautiful Russian Borzois,
were his constant companions, and he suggested to Scotty that it would be a good plan
to try the Dogs on the Bighorn.

Scotty grinned. "Guess you're from the
plains, pard. Wait till you see the kind of
place whar ole Krag hangs around."

# Krag, the Kootenay Ram

## XIV

WHERE the Yak-in-i-kak River leaves its parent
mountains, south of Gunder Peak, it comes
from a tremendous gorge called Skinkler's
Gulch. This is a mere crack in the vast granite hill, but is at least five hundred feet in depth.
Southward from the back of Gunder Peak is a
broken upland that runs to a point at this cañon,
and ends in a long promontory over the raging
walled-in stream.

This upland is good Sheep range, and by a
strange chance Scotty, coming up there with
Lee and the three Wolf-hounds, got a glimpse
of the Gunder Ram. The men kept out of
sight and hurried along by the hollows toward
the spot. But it was the old story. No sign
of their quarry. They found his great hoof-
mark just where they had seen him, so it was
no illusion; but the hard rocks about refused
further information, and no doubt Scotty would
have had another mysterious disappearance to
add to his list, but that the Dogs, nosing about
in all of the near hollows and thickets of dwarf
birch, broke out suddenly into a loud clamor,

70

and as they did so, up jumped a huge, gray, white-sterned animal—the Ram, the wonderful Gunder Ram. Over the low bushes, over the broken rocks, bounding, soaring, floating, supple, certain, splendid, he bore the great curling wonders on his head as lightly as a lady might her ear-rings; and then, from various other coverts, sprang up his band and joined him. Up flew the rifles; but in a moment the three great Dogs, closing in, gave unwitting screen to the one victim on which every thought was fixed, and not a shot was heard. Away they went, the Ram forging quickly to the lead, and the others stringing along after. Over the upland, flying, sailing, leaping, and swerving, they went. Over the level plains the Dogs would soon have caught the hindmost or perhaps their noblest prey, but on the rugged rocks it was clear that the Sheep were gaining. The men ran, one to the right, the other to the left, the better to keep sight; and Krag, cut off from the peak, dashed southward over the bench-land. Now it was a straight race. On it went —on, southward. The Dogs gained, and were near catching the hindmost Sheep; then it seemed that the Ram dropped back and now ran the rearmost. A rugged stretch was reached, and there the Sheep gained steadily, though little. One, two, three miles, and the chase was sweeping along the rocky ridge that ends in the sudden gash of Skinkler's Gulch. A minute more and the crowd of Sheep were rounded up and cornered on the final rock. They huddled together in terror, five hundred feet of dizzy cañon all around, three fierce Dogs and two fiercer men behind. Then, a few seconds later, old Krag dashed up. Cornered at last, he wheeled to fight; for the wild thing never yields.

He was now so far from the bounding Dogs that two rifle-balls whistled near. Of the Dogs he had no fears—them he could fight; but the rifles were sure death. There was one chance left. The granite walls of the Yak-in-i-kak could prove no harder than the human foe. The Dogs were within forty rods now, fine courageous animals, keen for fight, fearless of death; and behind, the hunters, remorseless and already triumphant. Sure death from them, or doubtful life in the gulch. There was no time

to hesitate; he, the leader, must act. He
wheeled to the edge, and *leaped*—down—down,
not to the bottom, not blindly. Thirty feet
downward, across the dizzy chasm, was a little
jut of rock, no bigger than his nose—the only
one in sight, all the rest smooth, sheer, or overhanging. But Krag landed fairly, poised just
a heart-beat. In a flash his blazing eyes took in
another point, his only hope, on the other side,
hidden under the overhanging rocks he had
leaped from. His supple loins and corded
limbs bent, pulsed, and floated him across, there
got fresh guidance to his flight, then back, sometimes to a mere roughness of the rock, on which
his hoofs, of horn and rubber built, gripped
for an instant, and took fresh ricochet to another
point. Then sidewise fifteen feet, and down,
down with modulated impact from point to
point, till, with a final drop of twenty feet, he
reached a ledge of safety far below.

And the others, inspired by his example, followed fast—a long cascade of Sheep. Had he
failed at one point all must have failed. But
now they came down headlong. It was splendid, it was inspiring! Hop, skip, down they

73

came, one after the other, now ten, now twenty feet, first to last leaping, sailing, bounding from point to ledge, from ledge to point, with masterly command of thew and hoof, with marvellous poise, and absolute success.

BUT just as the last had reached the second slender, speck-like foothold for its life, three white-and-yellow creatures whirled past her in the air, with gurgled gasps of horror, to perish far below.  The Hounds, impetuous and brave, never hesitated to follow a foe, and never knew how far more gifted was that foe than themselves until it was too late.  Down below, almost at the water's edge, Krag paused at length. Far above he heard the yells and whistles of the hunters; below in the boiling Yak-in-i-kak he saw a battered white-and-yellow form being hurried to the sea.

Lee and Scotty stood blankly at the edge. Sheep and Dogs had vanished; no possibility of escape for any.  Scotty uttered words that had no bearing on the case, only they were harsh, blasphemous words, and seemed to be necessary. Lee had a choking feeling in his throat, and he

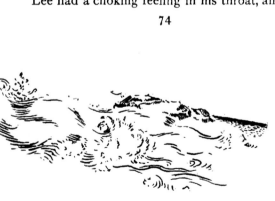

felt as no man can comprehend who has not lost a noble Dog by a sudden, tragic, and untimely end.

"Bran! Rollo! Ida!" he called in lingering hope; but the only response was from the Western Wind, that "snoofed" and whistled as it swept down Skinkler's Gulch.

## XV

LEE was a young, warm-hearted, impulsive cattle-man. For a day or two he hung about the shanty. The loss of his three friends was a sad blow: he had no heart for more mountaineering. But a few days later a spell of bracing weather helped his spirits, and he agreed when Scotty suggested a hunt. They reached the upper level, when Scotty, who had from time to time been scanning the hills with his glass, suddenly exclaimed:

"H—l! If thar ain't the old Gunder Ram. Thought he was smashed in Skinkler's Gulch!" and he sat down in amazement. Lee took the glass, and he recognized the wonderful Ram by his superb horns. The color rushed to the young

75

man's face. Now was his chance for glory and revenge at once! "Poor old Bran! good Rollo and Ida!"

Few animals have cunning enough to meet the combined drive and ambush. Scotty knew the lay of the land as well as the habits of the Ram.

"He ain't a-goin' to run down the wind, and he ain't a-goin' to quit the rocks. That means he'll pass up by the Gunder Peak, if he moves at all, an' he must take one side or the other. He won't go the west side if I show meself once that ar way. So you take the east; I'll give you two hours to get placed. I've a notion he'll cross the spur by that ledge."

Lee set out for his post. Scotty waited two hours, then moved on to a high ridge, and, clear against the sky, he waved his arms and walked up and down a few times. The Ram was not in sight, but Scotty knew he would see.

Then the old mountaineer circled back by hidden ways to the south, and began to walk and cut over the ridges toward the place where the Ram had been. He did not expect to see old Krag, but he did expect the Ram to see him. Lee was at his post, and, after a brief spell, he sighted the great Ram himself, bounding lightly down a ridge a mile away, and close behind him were three Ewes. They disappeared down a pine-clad hollow, and when they reappeared on the next ridge they were running as though in great alarm, their ears laid back; and from the hollow behind came, not, as Lee expected, the crack of Scotty's rifle or the sound of his yell, but the hunting chorus of Timber Wolves. Among the rocks the Sheep could easily escape, but among the timber or on the level such as now lay ahead, the advantage was with the Wolves; and a minute later these swept up in sight—five shaggy, furry brutes. The level open was crossed at whirling speed. The Sheep, racing for their lives, soon lengthened out into a procession in order of speed: far ahead the great Ram; behind him, with ten-yard gaps between them, the three Ewes; and forty yards behind the last, the five grim Wolves, closing, gaining at every leap. The bench-land narrowed eastward to pass a rocky shoulder. Long years and countless perils had taught the Sheep that in the rocks was safety, and that way led the Ram.

77

## Krag, the Kootenay Ram

But in the tangled upland birch the last of the
Ewes was losing ground; she gasped a short
*baah* as, thrown by a curling root, she lost a
few more precious yards. The Wolves were
almost within leaping distance when Krag
reached the shoulder-ledge. But a shoulder
above means a ravine below. In a moment,
at that call of distress, Krag wheeled on the
narrow ledge and faced the foe. He stood to
one side, and the three Ewes leaped past him and
on to safety. Then on came the Wolves, with
a howl of triumph. Many a Sheep had they
pulled down, and now they knew they soon
would feast. Without a pause they closed, but
in such a narrow pass, it was one at a time. The
leader sprang; but those death-dealing fangs
closed only on a solid mass of horn, and back of
that was a force that crushed his head against
himself, and dashed him at his friend behind
with such a fearful vim that both were hurled
over the cliff to perish on the rocks. On came
the rest. The Ram had no time to back up for
a charge, but a sweep of that great head was
enough. The points, forefronting now, as they
did when he was a Lamb, speared and hurled

78

F            Krag Wheeled and Faced the Foe.

the next Wolf, and the next; and then Krag
found a chance to back up and gather his
force. None but a mad Wolf could have failed
to take warning; but on he came, and Krag, in
savage glory of the fight, let loose that living
thunderbolt,—himself,—and met the last of the
furry monsters with a shock that crushed him
flat against the rock, then picked him up on his
horns as he might a rag, and hurled him farthest
yet, and standing on the edge he watched him
whirl and gasp till swallowed in the chasm.

The great Ram raised his splendid head,
blew a long blast from his nostrils, like a war-
horse, and gazed a moment to see if more were
coming; then turned and lightly bounded after
the Ewes he had so ably guarded.

From his hiding-place young Lee took in the
whole scene with eager, sparkling eyes. Only
fifty yards away from him it had passed.

He was an easy mark—fifty yards, standing;
he was a splendid mark, all far beyond old
Scotty's wildest talk. But Lee had seen a deed
that day that stirred his blood. He felt no
wish to end that life, but sat with brightened
eyes, and said with fervor: "You grand old

warrior! I do not care if you did kill my Dogs. You did it fair. I'll never harm you. For me, you may go in safety."

But the Ram never knew; and Scotty never understood.

## XVI

THERE was once a wretch who, despairing of other claims to notice, thought to achieve a name by destroying the most beautiful building on earth. This is the mind of the head-hunting sportsman. The nobler the thing that he destroys, the greater the deed, the greater his pleasure, and the greater he considers his claim to fame.

During the years that followed more than one hunter saw the great Ram and feasted his covetous eyes on his unparalleled horns. His fame even reached the cities. Dealers in the wonderful offered fabulous prices for the head that bore them—set blood-money on the life that grew them; and many came to try their luck, and failed. Then Scotty, always needy, was fired by a yet larger money offer, and setting out with his partner, they found the Ram,

with his harem about him. But in three days
of hard following they never got a second
glimpse; and the partner "reckoned thar was
easier money to git," and returned home.

But back of Scotty's sinister gray eyes was
the fibre of dogged persistency that has made
his race the masters of the world. He returned
with Mitchell to the shanty, but only to prepare
for a long and obstinate hunt. His rifle, his
blanket, his pipe, with matches, tobacco, a pot,
a bundle of jerked venison, and three or four
pounds of chocolate were all he carried. He
returned alone next day to the place where he
had left the track of the Ram, and followed it
fast in the snow, winding about, in and out, and
obscured by those of his band, but always dis-
tinguishable by its size. Once or twice Scotty
came on the spots where the band had been
lying down, and from time to time he scanned
the distance with his glass. But he saw nothing
of them. At night he camped on their trail;
next day he took it up again. After following
for hours, he came on the place where evidently
the Ram had stopped to watch him afar, and
so knew of his pursuer. Thenceforth the trail

# Krag, the Kootenay Ram

of the band for a long time was a single line as they headed for distant pastures.

Scotty followed doggedly behind; all day he followed, and at night, in a little hollow, crouched like a wild beast in his lair, with this difference only: he had a fire, and he smoked a pipe in very human fashion. In the morning he went on as before. Once or twice in the far distance he saw the band of Sheep travelling steadily southward. Next day passed, and the Sheep were driven to the south end of the Yak-in-i-kak range, just north of Whitefish Lake.

South of this was the Half-moon Prairie, east the broken land that stretched toward the north fork of the Flathead, and north of them their pertinacious and deadly foe. The Sheep were in doubt now, and as old Krag sought to sneak back by the lower benches of the east slope, he heard a " crack!" and a stinging something touched one horn and tore the hair from his shoulder.

The touch of a rifle-ball on the horn of a Ram has a more or less stunning effect; and Krag, dazed for a moment, gave the signal which in

84

our speech is, " Every one for himself now ";
and so the band was scattered. Some went this
way and some that, running more or less openly.

But Scotty's one thought was old Krag: he
heeded no other; and when the Ram made
straight away eastward down the hill, Scotty
again took up his trail, and cursed and
gasped as he followed.

The Flathead River was only a few miles
away. The Ram crossed on the ice, and keeping the roughest ground, turning when the wind
turned, he travelled all day northeastward, with
Scotty steadily behind. On the fifth day they
passed near Terry's Lake. Scotty knew the
ground. The Ram was going east, and would
soon run into a lot of lumber-camps; then turn
he must, for the region was a box canon; there
was only one way out. Scotty quit the trail,
and crossing northward to this one defile, down
which the Ram must go, he waited. The
West—the Chinook—Wind had been rising for
an hour or more, the one damp wind of the Rockies, the Snow Wind of the Hills; and as it rose
the flakes began to fly. In half an hour more
it was a blinding snow-storm. Things twenty

yards away were lost to view. But it did not last; the heaviest of it was over in a few minutes, and in two hours the skies were clear again. Scotty waited another hour, but seeing nothing, he left his post and searched about for sign; and found it, too—a dimpling row of tracks, much hidden by the recent snow, but clear in one place under a ledge. The Ram had passed unseen, had given him the slip, saved by the storm-wind and the snow.

Oh, Chinook! Mother West Wind! that brings the showers of spring and the snows of winter; that makes the grass grow on these great rolling uplands; that sustains the grass and all flesh that the grass sustains; that carved these uplands themselves, as well as made all things that live upon them—are you only a puff of air, or are you, as Greek and Indian both alike have taught, a something better, a living, thinking thing, that first creates, then loves and guards its own? Why did you come that day and hold your muffler about the eyes of the wolfish human brute, if it were not that you meant he should not see or harm your splendid dear one as he passed?

And was there not purpose in the meeting of

these very two, that you brought about long years ago, the day the Ram was born?

## XVII

Now Scotty thought there must be an object in the Ram's bold dash for the east side of the Flathead, and that object must be to reach the hills around Kintla Lake, on which he was well known and had many times been seen. He might keep west all day to-day, while the Chinook blew, but if the wind changed in the night he would surely turn eastward. So Scotty made no further attempt to keep the trail, or to make the west point of the Kintla Range, but cut straight northward over the divide toward the lake. The wind did change in the night. And next day, as Scotty scanned the vast expanse between him and the lake, he saw a moving speck below. He quickly got out of sight, then ran to intercept the traveller. But when he got to the spot he aimed at, and cautiously peered, there, five hundred yards away, on the next ridge, he stood—the famous Ram. Each was in plain view of the other.

Scotty stood for a minute and gazed in silence.

# Krag, the Kootenay Ram

Then, "Wal, ole Krag, ye kin see the skull and cross-bones on my gun. I'm Death on yer track; ye can't shake me off. At any price, I mean to have them horns. And here's for luck." Then he raised the rifle and fired; but the distance was great. The Ram stood till he saw the puff of smoke, then moved quickly to one side, and the snow was tossed by the ball not far from his former stand.

The Ram turned and made eastward, skirting the rugged southern shore of the lake, making for the main divide; and Scotty, left far behind for a time, trudged steadily, surely, behind him. For added to his tireless strength was the Saxon understreak of brutish grit, of senseless, pig-dogged pertinacity—the inflexible determination that still sticks to its purpose long after sense, reason, and honor have abandoned the attempt, that blinds its owner to his own defeat, and makes him, even when he is downed, still feebly strike—yes, spend his final mite of strength in madly girding at his conqueror, whose quick response, he knows, will be to wipe him out.

It was on, on, all day; then camp for the

night, and up again in the morning. Sometimes
the trail was easy to follow, sometimes blotted
out by new-fallen snow. But day after day
they went. Sometimes Scotty was in sight of
the prize that he pertinaciously was hunting,
but never very near. The Ram seemed to have
learned that five hundred yards was the farthest
range of the rifle, and allowed the man to come
up to that, the safety limit. After a time it
seemed as though he much preferred to have
him there, for then he knew where he was.
One time Scotty stole a march, and would have
had a close shot had not the fateful West Wind
borne the taint, and Krag was warned in time;
but this was in the first month of that dogged,
fearful following. After a while the Ram was
never out of sight.

Why did he not fly far away, and baffle the
hunter by his speed? *Because he must feed.*
The man had his dried venison and chocolate,
enough for many days; and when they were gone
he could shoot a hare or a grouse, hastily cook it,
and travel all day on that. But the Ram required
hours to seek the scanty grass under the snow.
The long pursuit was telling on him. His eyes

were blazing bright as ever, his shapely corded limbs as certain in their stride; but his belly was pinching up, and hunger, weakening hunger, was joining with his other foe.

For five long weeks the chase went on, and the only respite to the Gunder Ram was when some snow-storm from the west would interpose its veil.

Then came two weeks when they were daily in sight of each other. In the morning Scotty, rising wolf-like from his frosty lair, would call out, "Come, Krag; time we wuz a-movin'." And the Ram on the distant ridge would stamp defiantly, then, setting his nose to the wind, move on, now fast, now slow, but keeping ever the safe five hundred yards or more ahead. When Scotty sat down to rest the Ram would graze. If Scotty hid, the Ram would run in alarm to some place where near approach unseen would be impossible. If Scotty remained still for some time, the Ram would watch him intently and as still as himself. Thus they went on, day after day, till ten eventless weeks dragged slowly by. A singular feeling had grown up between the two. The Ram became so used to the sleuth-hound on his track that he accepted him as an inevitable, almost a necessary evil; and one day, when Scotty rose and scanned the northern distance for the Ram, he heard the long snort far behind, and turning, he saw old Krag impatiently waiting. The wind had changed, and Krag had changed his route to suit. One day after their morning's start Scotty had a difficult two hours in crossing a stream over which old Krag had leaped. When he did reach the other side he heard a snort, and looked around to find that the Ram had come back to see what was keeping him.

Oh, Krag! Oh, Gunder Ram! Why do you make terms with such a foe implacable? Why play with Death? Have all the hundred warnings of the Mother Wind been sent in vain? Keep on, keep on; do your best, that she may save you yet; but make no terms. Remember that the snow, which ought to save, may yet betray.

### XVIII

THUS in the winter all the Chief Mountain was traversed; the Kootenay Rockies, spur by spur, right up to the Crow's Nest Pass; then westward, in the face of the White Wind, the indomitable pair turned their steps, west and south to the McDonald Range; and onward still, till the Galtom Range was reached. Day by day the same old mechanical following—two dark moving specks on the great expanse of snow. Many a time their trail was crossed by that of other Sheep and other game. Once they met a party of miners who knew of Scotty and his hunt, and they chaffed him now; but he stared blankly, heeded them not, and went on. Many a time the Ram sought to hide his fateful footprints in the wake of some passing herd. But Scotty was not to be balked; his purpose had become his nature. All puzzles he worked out, and now there were fewer interruptions of the chase, for the snow-storms seemed to cease, the White Wind held aloof, and Nature offered no rebuke.

On and on, still the same scant half-mile apart; and on them both the hands of Time and Death seemed laid. Both were growing hollow-eyed and were gaunter every day. The man's hair had bleached since he set out on this in-

92

sane pursuit, and the head and shoulders of the
Ram were grizzling; only his jewel eyes and his
splendid sweeping horns were the same, and
borne as proudly as when first the chase began.

Each morning the man would rise,—stiff, half
frozen, and gaunt, but dogged as a very Hound
infernal,—and sneak along, trying for a close
shot. But always Krag was warned in time,
and springing into view from his own couch,
would lead the chase as before. Till in the
third month they crossed again from Galtom to
Tobacco Range, then eastward back to Gunder
Peak—the Ram, and the sleuth inexorable upon
his trail behind him. Here, on the birthplace of
the Ram, they sat one morning, at rest—the Ram
on one ridge, Scotty six hundred yards away
on the next. For twelve long weeks the Ram
had led him through the snow, over ten long
mountain-ranges—five hundred rugged miles.

And now they were back to their starting-
point, each with his lifetime wasted by one half
in that brief span. Scotty sat down, and lit
his pipe. The Ram made haste to graze.
As long as the man stayed there in view the
Ram would keep that ridge. Scotty knew

this well; a hundred times he had proved it. Then, as he sat and smoked, some evil spirit entered in and sketched a cunning plot. He emptied his pipe deliberately, put it away, then cut some rods of the low-creeping birch behind him; he gathered some stones; and the great Ram watched afar. The man moved to the edge of the ridge, and with sticks, some stones, and what clothing he could spare, he made a dummy of himself. Then, keeping exactly behind it, he crawled backward over the ledge and disappeared. After an hour of crawling and stalking he came up on a ridge behind the Ram.

There he stood, majestic as a bull, graceful as a deer, with horns that rolled around his brow like thunder-clouds about a peak. He was gazing intently on the dummy, wondering why his follower was so long still. Scotty was nearly three hundred yards away. Behind the Ram were some low rocks, but between was open snow. Scotty lay down and threw snow on his own back till he was all whitened, then set out to crawl two hundred yards, watching the great Ram's head, and coming on as fast as he dared. Still old Krag stared at the dummy,

94

sometimes impatiently stamping. Once he looked about sharply, and once he would have seen that deadly crawler in the snow, but that his horn itself, his great right horn, must interpose its breadth between his eye and his foe, and so his last small chance of escape was gone. Nearer, nearer to the sheltering rocks crawled the Evil One. Then, safely reaching them at last, he rested, a scant half-hundred yards away. For the first time in his life he saw the famous horns quite close. He saw the great, broad shoulders, the curving neck, still massive, though the mark of famine was on all; he saw this splendid fellow-creature blow the hot breath of life from his nostrils, vibrant in the sun; and he even got a glimpse of the life-light in those glowing amber eyes: but he slowly raised the gun.

Oh, Mother White Wind, only blow! Let not this be. Is all your power offset? Are not a million idle tons of snow on every peak awaiting? And one, just one, will do; a single flying wreath of snow will save him yet. The noblest living thing on all these hills, must he be stricken down to glut the basest lust of man? Because he erred but once, must he be doomed?

95

# Krag, the Kootenay Ram

But never day was calmer. Sometimes the Mountain Magpies warn their friends, but not a Bird was anywhere in view; and still the Gunder Ram was spellbound, watching that enemy, immovable, across the dip.

Up went the gun that never failed—directed by the eye that never erred. But the hand that had never trembled taking twenty human lives now shook as though in fear.

Two natures? Yes.

But the hand grew steady; the hunter's face was calm and hard. The rifle rang, and Scotty —hid his head; for the familiar "crack!" had sounded as it never did before. He heard a rattling on the distant stones, then a long-drawn *snoof!* But he neither looked nor moved. Two minutes later all was still, and he timidly raised his head. Was he gone? or what?

There on the snow lay a great gray-brown form, and at one end, like a twin-necked hydra coiling, were the horns, the wonderful horns, the sculptured record of the splendid life of a splendid creature, his fifteen years of life made visible at once. There were the points, much

96

worn now, that once had won his Lamb-days'
fight.   There were the years of robust growth,
each long in measure of that growth.   Here
was that year of sickness, there the splinter
on the fifth year's ring, which notched his
first love-fight.   The points had now come
round, and on them, could we but have seen,
were the lives of many Gray Wolves that had
sought his life.   And so the rings read on, the
living record of a life whose very preciousness
had brought it to a sudden end.

The golden chain across the web of white
was broken for its gold.

Scotty walked slowly over, and gazed in
sullen silence, not at the dear-won horns, but
at the calm yellow eyes, unclosed, and yet
undimmed by death.   Stone-cold was he.   He
did not understand himself.   He did not know
that this was the sudden drop after the long,
long slope up which he had been forcing himself for months.   He sat down twenty yards
away, with his back to the horns.   He put a
quid of tobacco in his mouth.   But his mouth
was dry; he spat it out again.   He did not
know what he himself felt.   Words played but

little part in his life, and his lips uttered only a torrent of horrid blasphemies, his one emotional outburst.

A long silence; then, "I'd give it back to him if I could."

He stared at the distance. His eyes fell on the coat he had left, and realizing that he was cold, he walked across and gathered up his things. Then he returned to the horns, and over him came the wild, inhuman lusting for his victim's body that he had heard his comrades speak of, but had never before understood—the reactionary lust that makes the panther fondle and caress the deer he has stricken down. He made a fire; then, feeling more like himself, he skinned the Ram's neck and cut off the head. This was familiar work, and he followed it up mechanically, cutting meat enough to satisfy his hunger. Then, bowing his shoulders beneath the weight of his massive trophy,—a weight he would scarcely have noticed three months ago,—he turned from the chase, old, emaciated, grizzled, and haggard, and toiled slowly down to the shanty he had left twelve weeks before.

## XIX

" No! Money couldn't buy it "; and Scotty
turned sullenly away to end discussion. He
waited a time till the taxidermist had done his
best, then he retraversed three hundred miles
of mountain to his lonely home. He removed
the cover, and hung the head where it got the
best light. The work was well done : the horns
were unchanged; the wonderful golden eyes
were there, and when a glint of light gave to
them a semblance of regard, the mountaineer
felt once more some of the feelings of that day
on the ridge. He covered up the head again.

Those who knew him best say he kept it
covered and never spoke about it. But one
man said : " Yes; I saw him uncover it once,
and look kind o' queer." The only remark he
ever made about it was : " Them's my horns,
but he'll get even with me yet."

Four years went by. Scotty, now known as
Old Man Scotty, had never hunted since. He
had broken himself down in that long madness..
He lived now entirely by his gold-pan, was
quite alone, and was believed to have something

on his mind. One day, late in the winter, an old partner stopped at his shanty. Their hours of conversation did not amount to as many paragraphs.

"I heared about ye killin' the Gunder Ram."

Scotty nodded.

"Let's see him, Scotty."

"Suit yourself"; and the old man jerked his head toward the draped thing on the wall. The stranger pulled off the cloth, and then followed the usual commonplace exclamations of wonder. Scotty received them in silence; but he turned to look. The firelight reflected in the glassy eyes lent a red and angry glare.

"Kivver him up when you're through," said Scotty, and turned to his smoking.

"Say, Scotty, why don't ye sell him if he bothers ye that-a-way? That there New-Yorker told me to tell ye that he'd give—"

"To h—l with yer New-Yorker! I'll niver sell him—I'll niver part with him. I stayed by him till I done him up, an' he'll stay by me till he gits even. He's been a-gittin' back at me these four years. He broke me down on that trip. He's made an old man o' me. He's left

me half luny. He's sucking my life out now.
But he ain't through with me yet. Thar's more
o' him round than that head. I tell ye, when
that old Chinook comes a-blowin' up the Ter-
bak-ker Crik, I've heared noises that the wind
don't make. I've heared him just the same as I
done that day when he blowed his life out
through his nose, an' me a-layin' on my face
afore him. I'm up ag'in' it, an' I'm a-goin' to
face it out—right—here—on—Ter-bak-ker—
Crik."

The White Wind rose high that night, and
hissed and wailed about Scotty's shanty. Ordinarily the stranger might not have noticed it;
but once or twice there came in over the door
a long *snoof* that jarred the latch and rustled vio-
lently the drapery of the head. Scotty glanced
at his friend with a wild, scared look. No
need for a word; the stranger's face was white.

In the morning it was snowing, but the
stranger went his way. All that day the White
Wind blew, and the snow came down harder
and harder. Deeper and deeper it piled on
everything. All the smaller peaks were rounded
off with snow, and all the hollows of the higher

ridges levelled.  Still it came down, not drifting, but piling up, heavy, soft, adhesive—all day long, deeper, heavier, rounder.  As night came on, the Chinook blew yet harder.  It skipped from peak to peak like a living thing—no puff of air, but a living thing, as Greek and Indian both alike have taught, a being who creates, then loves and guards its own.  It came like a mighty goddess, like an angry angel with a bugle-horn, with a dreadful message from the far-off western sea—a message of war; for it sang a wild, triumphant battle-song, and the strain of the song was:

> I am the mothering White Wind;
>   This is my hour of might.
> The hills and the snow are my children;
>   My service they do to-night.

And here and there, at the word received, there were mighty doings among the peaks. Here new effects were carven with a stroke; here lakes were made or unmade; here messengers of life and death despatched.  An avalanche from Purcell's Peak went down to gash the sides and show long veins of gold;

another hurried, by the White Wind sent, to block a stream and turn its wasted waters to a thirsty land—a messenger of mercy. But down the Gunder Peak there whirled a monstrous mass, charged with a mission of revenge. Down, down, down, loud *snoofing* as it went, and sliding on from shoulder, ledge, and long incline, now wiping out a forest that would bar its path, then crashing, leaping, rolling, smashing over cliff and steep descent, still gaining as it sped. Down, down, faster, fiercer, in one fell and fearful rush, and Scotty's shanty, in its track, with all that it contained, was crushed and swiftly blotted out. The hunter had forefelt his doom. The Ram's own Mother White Wind, from the western sea, had come— had long delayed, but still had come at last.

VER the rocky upland dawned the spring, over the level plain of Tobacco Creek. Gently the rains from the westward washed the great white pile of the snow-slide. Slowly the broken shanty came to light; and there in the middle, quite unharmed, was the head of the Gunder Ram.

103

## Krag, the Kootenay Ram

His amber eyes were gleaming bright as of old, under cover of those wonderful horns; and below him were some broken bones, with rags and grizzled human hair.

Old Scotty is forgotten, but the Ram's head hangs enshrined on a palace wall to-day, a treasure among kingly treasures; and men, when they gaze on those marvellous horns, still talk of the glorious Gunder Ram who grew them far away on the heights of the Kootenay.

Krag.

# A Street Troubadour:
## Being the Adventures of a Cock Sparrow

# A Street Troubadour :
## Being the Adventures of a Cock Sparrow

### I

UCH a chirruping, such a twittering, and such a squirming, fluttering mass! Half a dozen English Sparrows rolling over and chattering around one another in the Fifth Avenue gutter, and in the middle of the mob, when it scattered somewhat, could be seen the cause of it all—a little Hen Sparrow, vigorously, indignantly defending herself against her crowd of noisy suitors. They seemed to be making love to her, but their methods were so rough they might have been a lynching party. They plucked, worried, and harried the indignant little lady in a manner utterly disgraceful, ex-

cept that it was noticeable they did her no serious harm. She, however, laid about her with a will. Under no compulsion to spare her tormentors, apparently she would have slaughtered them all if she could.

It seemed clear that they were making love to her, but it seemed equally clear that she wanted none of them, and having partly convinced them of this at the point of her beak, she took advantage of a brief scattering of the assailants to fly up to the nearest eaves, displaying in one wing, as she went, some white feathers that afforded a mark to know her by, and may have been one of her chief charms.

## II

A Cock Sparrow, in the pride of his black cravat and white collar-points, was hard at work building in a bird-house that some children had set on a pole in the garden for such as he. He was a singular Bird in several respects. The building-material that he selected was all twigs, that must have been brought from Madison or Union Square, and in the early morning he

## A Street Troubadour

sometimes stopped work for a minute to utter a loud sweet song, much like that of a Canary.

It is not usual for a Cock Sparrow to build alone. But then this was an unusual Bird. After a week he had apparently finished the nest, for the bird-house was crammed to the very door with twigs purloined from the municipal shade-trees. He had now more leisure for music, and astonished the people about by frequent rendering of his long, unsparrow-like ditty; and he might have gone down to history as an unaccountable mystery, but that a barber bird-fancier on Sixth Avenue supplied the missing chapters of his early life.

This man, it seems, had put a Sparrow's egg into the wicker basket-nest of his Canaries. The youngster had duly hatched, and had been trained by the foster-parents. Their specialty was song. He had the lungs and robustness of his own race. The Canaries had trained him well, and the result was a songster who made up in energy what he lacked in native talent. Strong and pugnacious, as well as musical, this vociferous roustabout had soon made himself master of the cage. He had no hesitation in

## A Street Troubadour

hammering into silence a Canary that he could not put down by musical superiority, and after one of these little victories his strains were so unusually good that the barber had a stuffed Canary provided for the boisterous musician to vanquish whenever he wished to favor some visitor with Randy's exultant pæans of victory. He worried into silent subjection all of the Canaries he was caged with, and when finally kept by himself nothing angered him more than to be near some voluble songster that he could neither silence nor get at.   On these occasions he forgot his music, and his own Sparrow nature showed in the harsh *chirrup, chirrup* that has apparently been developed to make itself appreciated in the din of street traffic.

By the time his black bib had appeared he had made himself one of the chief characters and quite the chief attraction of the barber-shop. But one day the shelf on which the bird-cages stood gave way. all the cages were dashed to the floor, and in the general smash many of the Birds escaped.   Among them was Randy, or, more properly, Bertrand, as this pugnacious songster was named after the famous Trouba-

## A Street Troubadour

dour.  The Canaries had voluntarily returned
to their cages, or permitted themselves to be
caught.  But Randy hopped out of a back win-
dow, chirruped a few times, sang a defiant answer to the elevated-railway whistle, and keeping
just out of reach of all attempts to capture him,
he began to explore the brick wilderness about.
He had not been a prisoner for generations.
He readily accepted the new condition of freedom, and within a week was almost as wild as
any of his kin, and had degenerated into a little
street rowdy like the others, squabbling among
them in the gutter, giving them blow for blow,
or surprising all hearers with occasional bursts
of Canary music delivered with Sparrow energy.

### III

THIS, then, was Randy, who had selected the
bird-house for a nesting-place, and the reason
for his intemperance in the matter of twigs is
now clear.  The only nest he had ever known
was of basketwork; therefore a proper nest is
made of twigs.

Within a few days Randy appeared with a

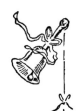

## A Street Troubadour

mate. I might have forgotten the riot scene in the gutter, as such things are common, but that I now recognized in Randy's bride the little white-winged Biddy Sparrow that had caused it.

She had apparently accepted Randy, but she was still putting on airs, pecking at him when he came near. He was squirming around with drooping wings and tilted tail, chirping like any other ardent Cock Sparrow, but occasionally stopping to show off his Canary accomplishment.

Any objections she may have had were apparently overcome, possibly by this astonishing display of genius, and he escorted her to the ready-made nest, running in ahead to show the way, and hopping proudly, noisily, officiously about her. She followed him, but came out again quickly, with Randy after her chirping and beseeching. He chattered a long time before he could persuade her to reënter, but again she came out immediately, this time sputtering and scolding. Again he seemed to exert his power of persuasion, and finally she went in chattering, reappeared with a twig in her bill, dropped it, and flew away out of sight. Randy came out.

# A Street Troubadour

All his joy and pride in his house were gone.
This was a staggering blow, when he had looked
for unmitigated commendation. He sat dis-
consolately on the door-step for a minute, and
chirruped in a way that probably meant, " Come
back, come back!" But his bride did not come.
He turned into the house. There was a scratching sound, and he came out at once with a large
stick and flung it from the door to the ground.
He returned for another, sent that flying after
the first, and so went on, dragging out and
hurling down all the sticks he had so carefully
and laboriously carried in. That wonderful
forked one that had given so much trouble to
get here from Union Square, and those two
smooth ones, just like the ones in his foster-
mother's nest—all, all must go. For over an
hour he toiled away in silence and alone. Then,
apparently, he had ended his task, for on the
ground below was a pile of sticks, as big as a
bonfire, the labor of a week undone. Randy
glared fiercely at them and at the empty house,
gave a short, harsh chirp, probably a Sparrow
bad word, then flew away.

Next day he reappeared with Biddy, fussing

about her in passerine exuberance once more, and chirping as he led her to the door again. She hopped in, then out, looked aslant at the twigs below, went back in, reappeared with a very small twig that had been overlooked, dropped it, and with evident satisfaction watched it fall on the pile below. After running in and out a dozen times they set off together, and presently returned, Biddy with her bill full of hay, Randy with one straw. These were carried in and presumably arranged satisfactorily. Then they went for more hay, and having got Randy set right, she remained in the box to arrange the hay as he brought it, only occasionally going for a load when he was long in coming. It was marvellous to see how the chivalry in this aggressive musician was reducing him to subjection. It seemed a good opportunity to try their tastes. I put out thirty short strings and ribbons in a row on a balcony near. Fifteen were common strips, eight were gaudy strips, and seven were bright silk ribbons. Every other one in the row was a dull string. Biddy was the first to see this array of material. She flew down, looked over it, around it, left eye,

A Street Troubadour

right eye; then decided to let it alone. But
Randy came closer; he was not unfamiliar with
threads. He hopped this way, then that, pulled
at a thread, started back, but came nearer,
nibbled at one or two, then made a dart at a
string and bore it away. Next time Biddy
came, and each bore off a string. They took
only the dull ones, but after these were gone
Biddy selected some of the brighter material,
though even she did not venture on the gaudiest
ribbons, and Randy would have no hand in
bringing home any but the soberest and most
stick-like materials. The nest was now half
done. Randy once more ventured to carry in a
stick, but a moment later it was whirling down
to the pile below, with Biddy triumphantly gazing after it. Poor Randy! no toleration for
*his* hobby—all those splendid sticks wasted.
His mother had had a stick nest,—a beautiful
nest it was,—but he was overruled. Nothing
but straw now; then, not sticks, but softer
material. He submitted—liberty had brought
daily lessons of submission. He used to think
that the barber-shop was the whole world and
himself the most important living being. But

117

of late both these ideas had been badly shaken. Biddy found that his education had been sadly neglected in all useful matters, and in each new kind of material she had to instruct him anew.

When the nest was two thirds finished, Biddy, whose ideas were quite luxurious, began to carry in large soft feathers. But now Randy thought this was going too far. He must draw the line somewhere. He drew it at feather beds. His earliest cradle had had no such lining. He proceeded to bundle out the objectionable feather bedding, and Biddy, returning with a new load, was just in time to see the first lot float downward from the door to join the stick pile below. She fluttered after them, seized them in the air, and returned to meet her lord coming out of the door with more of the obnoxious plumes, and there they stood, glaring at each other, chattering their loudest, their mouths full of feathers, and their hearts full of indignation.

How is it that when it is a question of home furnishing we sympathize with the female? I felt that Biddy had first right, and in the end she got her way. First there was a stormy

118

Randy Drew the Line at Feather Beds.

time in which quantities of feathers were carried
in and out of the house, or wind-borne about the
garden. Then there was a lull, and next day
all the feathers were carried back to the nest.
Just how they arranged the matter will never be
known, but it is sure that Randy himself did the
greater part of the work, and never stopped till
the box was crammed with the largest and softest of feathers. During all this they were usually together, but one day Biddy went off and
stayed for some time. Randy looked about,
chirruped, got no answer, looked up, then down,
and far below he saw the pile of sticks that he
had toiled to bring. Those dear sticks, just
like the home of his early days! Randy fluttered down. There was the curious forked one
still. The temptation was irresistible. Randy
picked it up and hurried to the nest, then in.
It had always been a difficult twig to manage
—that side prong would catch at the door; but
he had carried it so often now that he knew
how. After half a minute's delay inside, while
he was placing it, I suppose, he came out again,
looked perkily about, preened and shook himself, then sang his Canary song from beginning

to end several times, tried some new bars, and seemed extremely happy. When Biddy came with more feathers, he assiduously helped her to place them inside, and then the nest was finished. Two days later I got up to the nest, and in it found one egg. The Sparrows saw me go up, but did not fly chattering about my head, as do most Birds. They flew away to a distance, and watched anxiously from the shelter of some chimneys.

The third day there was a great commotion in the box, a muffled scuffling and chattering, and once or twice a tail appeared at the door as though the owner were trying to back out. Then it seemed that something was being dragged about. At length the owner of the tail came out far enough to show that it was Biddy; but, apparently, she was pulled in again. Evidently a disgraceful family brawl was on. It was quite unaccountable, until finally Biddy struggled out of the door, dragging Randy's pet twig to throw it contemptuously on the ground below. She had discovered it in the bedding where he had hidden it; hence the row. But I do not see how she could drag it out when he was

# A Street Troubadour

resisting.  I suspect that he really weakened for
the sake of peace.  In the scuffle and general
upset the egg—their first arrival—was unfortunately tumbled out with the stick, and fell down
to lie below, in porcelain fragments, on a wet
yellow background.  The Sparrows did not
seem to trouble about the remains.  Having
dropped from the nest, it had dropped out of
their world.

IV

AFTER this the pair got along peaceably for
several days.  Egg after egg was added to the
nest.  In a week there were five, and the two
seemed now to be quite happy together.  Randy
sang to the astonishment of all the neighborhood, and Biddy carried in more feathers as
though preparing to set and anticipating a blizzard.  But about this time it occurred to me to
try a little experiment with the pair.  Watching
my chance, late one evening, I dropped a
marble into the luxurious nest.  What happened
at once I do not know, but early the next morning I was out on Fifth Avenue near the corner
of Twenty-first Street.  It was Sunday.  The

123

## A Street Troubadour

street was very quiet, but a ring of perhaps a dozen people were standing gazing at something in the gutter. As I came near I heard occasional chirruping, and getting a view into the ring, I saw two Sparrows locked in fierce combat, chirruping a little, but hammering and pecking away in deadly earnest. They scuffled around, regardless of the bystanders, for some time ; but when at length they paused for breath, and sat back on their tails and heels to gasp, I was quite shocked to recognize Biddy and Randy. After another round they were shooed away by one of the onlookers, who evidently disapproved of Sunday brawling. They then flew to the nearest roof to go on as before. That afternoon I found below the nest not only the intrusive marble, but also the remains of the five eggs, all alike thrown out, and I suspect that the presence of that curious hard round egg in the nest, and the obvious implication, were the cause of the brawl.

Whether Biddy had been able to explain it or not I do not know, but it seemed that the couple decided to forget the past and begin again. There was evidently neither luck nor

## A Street Troubadour

peace in that bird-box, so they abandoned it, feathers and all; and Biddy, whose ideas were distinctly original, selected the site this time, nothing less than the top of an electric lamp in the middle of Madison Square. All week they labored, and in spite of a high wind most of the time, they finished the nest. It is hard to see how the Birds could sleep at night with that great glaring buzzing light under their noses. Still, Biddy seemed pleased, Randy was learning to suppress his own opinion, and all would have gone well but that before the first egg was laid the carbon-points of the light burned out, and the man who put in the new ones thought proper to consign remorselessly the whole of the Biddy-Randy mansion to the garbage-can. A Robin or a Swallow might have felt this a crushing blow, but there is no limit to a Sparrow's energy and hopefulness. Evidently it was the wrong kind of a nest. Probably the material was at fault. At any rate, a radical change would be much better. After embezzling some long straws from the nest of an absent neighbor, Biddy laid them in the high fork of an elm-tree in Madison Square Park, by way of letting

125

## A Street Troubadour

Randy know that this was the place now selected; and Randy, having learned by this time
that it was less trouble to accept her decision
than to offer an opinion of his own, sang a
Canary trill on two chirps, and set about rum-
maging in the garbage-heaps for choice building-
material, winking hard and looking the other
way when a nice twig presented itself.

V

On the other side of the Square was the nest of
a pair of very unpopular Sparrows. The male
bird in particular had made himself thoroughly
disliked. He was a big, handsome fellow with
an enormous black cravat, but an out-and-out
bully. Might is right in Sparrow world. Their
causes for quarrel are food, mates, quarters, and
nesting-material—pretty much as with our-
selves. This arrogant little Bird, by reason of his
strength, had the mate of his choice and the best
nesting-site, and was adding to it all the most-
admired material in the Square. My Sparrows
had avoided the gaudy ribbons I offered. They
were not educated up to that pitch, but they

126

certainly had their esthetic preferences. A few Guinea-fowl feathers that originally came from Central Park Menagerie had been stolen from one nest to another, till now they rested in the sumptuous home with which Cravat and his wife had embellished one of the marble capitals of the new bank. The Bully did much as he pleased in the Park, and one day, on hearing Randy's song, flew at him. Randy had been a terror among Canaries, but against Cravat he had but little chance. He did his best, but was defeated, and took refuge in flight. Puffed up by this victory, the Bully flew to Randy's new nest, and after a more or less scornful scrutiny proceeded to drag out some strings that he thought he might use at home. Randy had been worsted, but the sight of this pillage roused the doughty Troubadour again, and he flew at the Bully as before. From the branches they tumbled to the ground. Other Sparrows joined in, and, shame to tell! they joined with the big fellow against the comparative stranger. Randy was getting very roughly handled, feathers began to float away, when into the ring flashed a little Hen Sparrow with white wing-feathers, chirrup, chirrup, wallop, wallop, she went into it. Oh, how she did lay about her! The Sparrows that had joined in for fun now went off: there was no longer any fun in it, nothing but hard pecks, and the tables were completely turned on Cravat. He quickly lost heart, then, and fled toward his own quarter of the Square, with Biddy holding on to his tail like a little bulldog; and there she continued to hang till the feather came out by the roots, and she afterward had the satisfaction of working it into the coarser make-up of her nest along with the rescued material. It is hardly possible that Sparrows have refined ideas of justice and retribution, but it is sure that things which look like it do crop up among them. Within two days the Guinea-fowl feathers that had so long been the chief glory of the Cravat's nest now formed part of the furnishing of Biddy's new abode, and none had the temerity to dispute her claim.

It was now late in the season, feathers were scarce, and Biddy could not find enough for the lining that she was so particular about. But she found a substitute that appealed to her love

Drove Off the Bully.

of the novel. In the Square was the cab-stand, and scattering near were usually more or less horsehairs. These seemed to be good and original linings. A most happy thought, and with appropriate enthusiasm the ever-hopeful couple set about gathering horsehairs, two or three at a time. Possibly the nest of a Chipping Sparrow in one of the parks gave them the idea. The Chippy always lines with horsehair, and gets an admirable spring-mattress effect by curling the hair round and round the inside of the nest. The result is good, but one must know how to get it. It would have been well had the Sparrows learned how to handle the hair. When a Chippy picks up a horsehair to bring home it takes only one at a time, and is careful to lift it by the end, for the harmless-looking hair is not without its dangers. The Sparrows had no notion of handling it except as they did the straw. Biddy seized a hair near the middle, found it somewhat long, so took a second hold, several inches away. In most cases this made a great loop in the hair over her head or beyond her beak. But it was a convenient way to manage, and at first no mischief came,

131

though Chippy, had she seen, might well have shuddered at the idea of that threatening noose.

It was the last day of the lining. Biddy had in some way given Randy to understand that no more hair was needed, and, proud and bustling, she was adding a few finishing touches and a final hair while he was trying some new variations of his finest bars on top of Farragut's head, when a loud alarm chirrup from Biddy caught his ear. He looked toward the new home to see her struggling up and down without apparent reason, and yet unable to get more than her length away from the nest. She had at last put her head through one of those dangerous hair nooses, made by herself, and by mischance had tightened and twisted it so that she was caught. The more she struggled and twisted the tighter became the noose. Randy now discovered that he was deeply attached to this wilful little termagant. He became greatly excited, and flew about chattering. He tried to release her by pulling at her foot, but that only made matters worse. All their efforts were in vain. Several new kinks were added to the hair. Other hairs from the nest seemed to join in the plot, and, tangled and intermeshed, they tightened even more, till the group of wondering, upturned child faces in the Park below were centred on a tousled feathery form hanging still and silent in the place of the bustling, noisy, energetic Biddy Sparrow.

Poor Randy seemed deeply distressed. The neighbor Sparrows had come at the danger-call note, and joined their cries with his, but had not been able to help the victim. Now they went off to their own squabbles and troubles, and Randy hopped about chirping or sat still with drooping wings. It was long before he realized that she was dead, and all that day he exerted himself to interest her and make her join in their usual life. At night he rested alone in one of the trees, and at gray dawn was bustling about, singing occasionally and chirruping around the nest, from whose rim, in the fateful horsehair, hung Biddy, stiff and silent now.

## VI

RANDY had never been an alert Sparrow. His Canary training had really handicapped him.

## A Street Troubadour

He was venturesome and heedless with carriages
as well as with children. This peculiarity was
greatly increased by his present preoccupation,
and while foraging somewhat listlessly on Madison Avenue, that afternoon, a messenger-boy
on a wheel came silently up, and before Randy
realized his danger, the wheel was on his tail.
As he struggled to get away, even at the price
of his tail, his right wing flashed under the
hind wheel, and then he was crippled. The boy
rode on, and Randy managed to flutter and hop
away toward the sheltering trees. A little girl,
assisted by her small dog, captured the cripple,
after an exciting chase among the benches.
She took him home, and moved by what her
brothers considered sadly misplaced tenderness,
she caged and nursed him. When he began to
recover, he one day surprised them by singing
his Canary song.

This created quite a stir in the household.
In time a newspaper reporter heard of it. The
inevitable write-up followed, and this met the
eye of the Sixth Avenue barber. He came
with many witnesses to claim his bird, and at
length his claim was allowed.

134

# A Street Troubadour

So Randy is once more in a cage, carefully watched and fed, the central figure in a small world, and not at all unhappy. After all, he was never a truly wild Bird. It was an accident that set him free originally. An accident had mated him with Biddy. Their brief life together had been a succession of storms and accidents. An accident had taken her away, and another accident had renewed his cage life. This life, comparatively calm and uneventful, has given him an opportunity to cultivate his musical gifts, for he is in a very conservatory of music, and close at hand are his old tutors and foster-parents.

Sometimes when left alone he amuses himself by beginning a rude nest of sticks, but he looks guilty, and leaves that corner of the cage when any one comes near. If a few feathers are given him they are worked into the nest at first, but next morning are invariably found on the floor below. These persistent attempts at nesting suggested that he wanted a mate, and several were furnished on approval, but the result was not happy. Prompt interference was needed each time to prevent bloodshed and to

## A Street Troubadour

rescue the intended bride. So the attempt was given up. Evidently this Troubadour wants no new lady-love. His songs seem to be rather of war, for the barber has discovered that when he wishes to provoke Randy into his most rapturous musical expression it is only necessary to let him demolish, not the effigy of a Canary, but a stuffed Cock Sparrow. And on these occasions Randy develops an enthusiasm almost amounting to inspiration if the dummy have a very well marked black patch on the throat.

This, however, is mere by-play. All his best energies are devoted to song. And if you stumble on the right barber-shop you may see this energetic recluse, forgetting the cares, joys, and sorrows of active life in his devotion to music, like some monk who has tried the world, found it too hard for him, and has gladly returned to his cell, there to devote the rest of his days to purely spiritual pleasures.

Biddy and Randy.

Johnny Bear

# Johnny Bear

JOHNNY was a queer little Bear cub that lived with Grumpy, his mother, in the Yellowstone Park. They were among the many Bears that found a desirable home in the country about the Fountain Hotel.

The steward of the Hotel had ordered the kitchen garbage to be dumped in an open glade of the surrounding forest, thus providing, throughout the season, a daily feast for the Bears, and their numbers have increased each year since the law of the land has made the Park a haven of refuge where no wild thing may be harmed. They have accepted man's peace-

# Johnny Bear

offering, and many of them have become so well known to the Hotel men that they have received names suggested by their looks or ways. Slim Jim was a very long-legged thin Blackbear; Snuffy was a Blackbear that looked as though he had been singed; Fatty was a very fat, lazy Bear that always lay down to eat; the Twins were two half-grown, ragged specimens that always came and went together. But Grumpy and Little Johnny were the best known of them all.

Grumpy was the biggest and fiercest of the Blackbears, and Johnny, apparently her only son, was a peculiarly tiresome little cub, for he seemed never to cease either grumbling or whining. This probably meant that he was sick, for a healthy little Bear does not grumble all the time, any more than a healthy child. And indeed Johnny looked sick; he was the most miserable specimen in the Park. His whole appearance suggested dyspepsia; and this I quite understood when I saw the awful mixtures he would eat at that garbage-heap. Anything at all that he fancied he would try. And his mother allowed him to do as he

142

His Whole Appearance Suggested Dyspepsia.

# Johnny Bear

pleased ; so, after all, it was chiefly her fault, for she should not have permitted such things.

Johnny had only three good legs, his coat was faded and mangy, his limbs were thin, and his ears and paunch were disproportionately large. Yet his mother thought the world of him. She was evidently convinced that he was a little beauty and the Prince of all Bears, so, of course, she quite spoiled him. She was always ready to get into trouble on his account, and he was always delighted to lead her there. Although such a wretched little failure, Johnny was far from being a fool, for he usually knew just what he wanted and how to get it, if teasing his mother could carry the point.

## II

It was in the summer of 1897 that I made their acquaintance. I was in the Park to study the home life of the animals, and had been told that in the woods, near the Fountain Hotel, I. could see Bears at any time, which, of course, I scarcely believed. But on stepping out of the back door five minutes after arriving, I came

# Johnny Bear

face to face with a large Blackbear and her two cubs.

I stopped short, not a little startled. The Bears also stopped and sat up to look at me. Then Mother Bear made a curious short *Koff Koff*, and looked toward a near pine-tree. The cubs seemed to know what she meant, for they ran to this tree and scrambled up like two little monkeys, and when safely aloft they sat like small boys, holding on with their hands, while their little black legs dangled in the air, and waited to see what was to happen down below.

The Mother Bear, still on her hind legs, came slowly toward me, and I began to feel very uncomfortable indeed, for she stood about six feet high in her stockings and had apparently never heard of the magical power of the human eye.

I had not even a stick to defend myself with, and when she gave a low growl, I was about to retreat to the Hotel, although previously assured that the Bears have always kept their truce with man. However, just at this turning-point the old one stopped, now but thirty feet away, and

146

## Johnny Bear

continued to survey me calmly. She seemed in doubt for a minute, but evidently made up her mind that, "although that human thing might be all right, she would take no chances for her little ones."

She looked up to her two hopefuls, and gave a peculiar whining *Er-r-r Er-r*, whereupon they, like obedient children, jumped, as at the word of command. There was nothing about them heavy or bear-like as commonly understood; lightly they swung from bough to bough till they dropped to the ground, and all went off together into the woods. I was much tickled by the prompt obedience of the little Bears. As soon as their mother told them to do something they did it. They did not even offer a suggestion. But I also found out that there was a good reason for it, for had they not done as she had told them they would have got such a spanking as would have made them howl.

This was a delightful peep into Bear home life, and would have been well worth coming for, if the insight had ended there. But my friends in the Hotel said that that was not the

# Johnny Bear

best place for Bears. I should go to the gar-
bage-heap, a quarter-mile off in the forest.
There, they said, I surely could see as many
Bears as I wished (which was absurd of them).

Early the next morning I went to this Bears'
Banqueting Hall in the pines, and hid in the
nearest bushes.

Before very long a large Blackbear came
quietly out of the woods to the pile, and began
turning over the garbage and feeding. He was
very nervous, sitting up and looking about at
each slight sound, or running away a few yards
when startled by some trifle. At length he
cocked his ears and galloped off into the pines,
as another Blackbear appeared. He also be-
haved in the same timid manner, and at last ran
away when I shook the bushes in trying to get
a better view.

At the outset I myself had been very nervous, for of course no man is allowed to carry
weapons in the Park; but the timidity of these
Bears reassured me, and thenceforth I forgot
everything in the interest of seeing the great,
shaggy creatures in their home life.

Soon I realized I could not get the close in-

148

## Johnny Bear

sight I wished from that bush, as it was seventy-five yards from the garbage-pile. There was none nearer; so I did the only thing left to do: I went to the garbage-pile itself, and, digging a hole big enough to hide in, remained there all day long, with cabbage-stalks, old potato-peelings, tomato-cans, and carrion piled up in odorous heaps around me. Notwithstanding the opinions of countless flies, it was not an attractive place. Indeed, it was so unfragrant that at night, when I returned to the Hotel, I was not allowed to come in until after I had changed my clothes in the woods.

It had been a trying ordeal, but I surely did see Bears that day. If I may reckon it a new Bear each time one came, I must have seen over forty. But of course it was not, for the Bears were coming and going. And yet I am certain of this: there were at least thirteen Bears, for I had thirteen about me at one time.

All that day I used my sketch-book and journal. Every Bear that came was duly noted; and this process soon began to give the desired insight into their ways and personalities.

Many unobservant persons think and say that

149

all Negroes, or all Chinamen, as well as all animals of a kind, look alike. But just as surely as each human being differs from the next, so surely each animal is different from its fellow; otherwise how would the old ones know their mates or the little ones their mother, as they certainly do? These feasting Bears gave a good illustration of this, for each had its individuality; no two were quite alike in appearance or in character.

This curious fact also appeared : I could hear the Woodpeckers pecking over one hundred yards away in the woods, as well as the Chickadees chickadeeing, the Blue-jays blue-jaying, and even the Squirrels scampering across the leafy forest floor; and yet I *did not hear one of these Bears come.* Their huge, padded feet always went down in exactly the right spot to break no stick, to rustle no leaf, showing how perfectly they had learned the art of going in silence through the woods.

### III

ALL morning the Bears came and went or wandered near my hiding-place without dis-

# Johnny Bear

covering me; and, except for one or two brief quarrels, there was nothing very exciting to note. But about three in the afternoon it became more lively.

There were then four large Bears feeding on the heap. In the middle was Fatty, sprawling at full length as he feasted, a picture of placid ursine content, puffing just a little at times as he strove to save himself the trouble of moving by darting out his tongue like a long red serpent, farther and farther, in quest of the tidbits just beyond claw reach.

Behind him Slim Jim was puzzling over the anatomy and attributes of an ancient lobster. It was something outside his experience, but the principle, "In case of doubt take the trick," is well known in Bearland, and settled the difficulty.

The other two were clearing out fruit-tins with marvellous dexterity. One supple paw would hold the tin while the long tongue would dart again and again through the narrow opening, avoiding the sharp edges, yet cleaning out the can to the last taste of its sweetness.

This pastoral scene lasted long enough to be sketched, but was ended abruptly. My eye

151

caught a movement on the hilltop whence all the Bears had come, and out stalked a very large Blackbear with a tiny cub.  It was Grumpy and Little Johnny.

The old Bear stalked down the slope toward the feast, and Johnny hitched alongside, grumbling as he came, his mother watching him as solicitously as ever a hen did her single chick. When they were within thirty yards of the garbage-heap, Grumpy turned to her son and said something which, judging from its effect, must have meant: " Johnny, my child, I think you had better stay here while I go and chase those fellows away."

Johnny obediently waited ; but he wanted to *see*, so he sat up on his hind legs with eyes agog and ears acock.

Grumpy came striding along with dignity, uttering warning growls as she approached the four Bears.  They were too much engrossed to pay any heed to the fact that yet another one of them was coming, till Grumpy, now within fifteen feet, let out a succession of loud coughing sounds, and charged into them.  Strange to say, they did not pretend to face her, but, as

Old Grumpy Stalked Down the Slope, and
Johnny Hitched Alongside.

But Johnny Wanted to See.

soon as they saw who it was, scattered and all
fled for the woods.

Slim Jim could safely trust his heels, and the
other two were not far behind; but poor Fatty,
puffing hard and waddling like any other very
fat creature, got along but slowly, and, unluck-
ily for him, he fled in the direction of Johnny,
so that Grumpy overtook him in a few bounds
and gave him a couple of sound slaps in the
rear which, if they did not accelerate his pace, at
least made him bawl, and saved him by changing his direction. Grumpy, now left alone in
possession of the feast, turned toward her son
and uttered the whining *Er-r-r Er-r-r Er-r-r-r.*
Johnny responded eagerly. He came "hopity-
hop" on his three good legs as fast as he could,
and, joining her on the garbage, they began to
have such a good time that Johnny actually
ceased grumbling.

He had evidently been there before now, for
he seemed to know quite well the staple kinds
of canned goods. One might almost have supposed that he had learned the brands, for a
lobster-tin had no charm for him as long as he
could find those that once were filled with jam.

157

# Johnny Bear

Some of the tins gave him much trouble, as he was too greedy or too clumsy to escape being scratched by the sharp edges. One seductive fruit-tin had a hole so large that he found he could force his head into it, and for a few minutes his joy was full as he licked into all the farthest corners. But when he tried to draw his head out, his sorrows began, for he found himself caught. He could not get out, and he scratched and screamed like any other spoiled child, giving his mother no end of concern, although she seemed not to know how to help him. When at length he got the tin off his head, he revenged himself by hammering it with his paws till it was perfectly flat.

A large sirup-can made him happy for a long time. It had had a lid, so that the hole was round and smooth; but it was not big enough to admit his head, and he could not touch its riches with his tongue stretched out its longest. He soon hit on a plan, however. Putting in his little black arm, he churned it around, then drew out and licked it clean; and while he licked one he got the other one ready; and he did this again and again, until the can

158

A Sirup-tin Kept Him Happy for a Long Time.

## Johnny Bear

was as clean inside as when first it had left the factory.

A broken mouse-trap seemed to puzzle him. He clutched it between his fore paws, their strong inturn being sympathetically reflected in his hind feet, and held it firmly for study. The cheesy smell about it was decidedly good, but the thing responded in such an uncanny way, when he slapped it, that he kept back a cry for help only by the exercise of unusual self-control. After gravely inspecting it, with his head first on this side and then on that, and his lips puckered into a little tube, he submitted it to the same punishment as that meted out to the refractory fruit-tin, and was rewarded by discovering a nice little bit of cheese in the very heart of the culprit.

Johnny had evidently never heard of ptomaïne-poisoning, for nothing came amiss. After the jams and fruits gave out he turned his attention to the lobster- and sardine-cans, and was not appalled by even the army beef. His paunch grew quite balloon-like, and from much licking his arms looked thin and shiny, as though he was wearing black silk gloves.

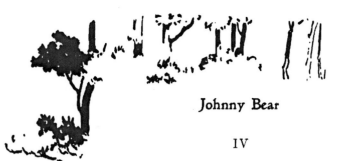

## Johnny Bear

### IV

It occurred to me that I might now be in a
really dangerous place. For it is one thing
surprising a Bear that has no family responsibilities, and another stirring up a bad-tempered
old mother by frightening her cub.

"Supposing," I thought, "that cranky Little
Johnny should wander over to this end of the
garbage and find me in the hole; he will at once
set up a squall, and his mother, of course, will
think I am hurting him, and, without giving me
a chance to explain, may forget the rules of the
Park and make things very unpleasant."

Luckily, all the jam-pots were at Johnny's
end; he stayed by them, and Grumpy stayed
by him. At length he noticed that his mother
had a better tin than any he could find, and as
he ran whining to take it from her he chanced
to glance away up the slope. There he saw
something that made him sit up and utter a
curious little *Koff Koff Koff Koff*.

His mother turned quickly, and sat up to see
"what the child was looking at." I followed
their gaze, and there, oh, horrors! was an

Johnny Got Behind his Mother.

# Johnny Bear

enormous Grizzly Bear. He was a monster; he looked like a fur-clad omnibus coming through the trees.

Johnny set up a whine at once and got behind his mother. She uttered a deep growl, and all her back hair stood on end. Mine did too, but I kept as still as possible.

With stately tread the Grizzly came on. His vast shoulders sliding along his sides, and his silvery robe swaying at each tread, like the trappings on an elephant, gave an impression of power that was appalling.

Johnny began to whine more loudly, and I fully sympathized with him now, though I did not join in. After a moment's hesitation Grumpy turned to her noisy cub and said something that sounded to me like two or three short coughs—*Koff Koff Koff.* But I imagine that she really said: "My child, I think you had better get up that tree, while I go and drive the brute away."

At any rate, that was what Johnny did, and this what she set out to do. But Johnny had no notion of missing any fun. He wanted to *see* what was going to happen. So he did not

## Johnny Bear

rest contented where he was hidden in the thick branches of the pine, but combined safety with view by climbing to the topmost branch that would bear him, and there, sharp against the sky, he squirmed about and squealed aloud in his excitement. The branch was so small that it bent under his weight, swaying this way and that as he shifted about, and every moment I expected to see it snap off. If it had been broken when swaying my way, Johnny would certainly have fallen on me, and this would probably have resulted in bad feelings between myself and his mother; but the limb was tougher than it looked, or perhaps Johnny had had plenty of experience, for he neither lost his hold nor broke the branch.

Meanwhile, Grumpy stalked out to meet the Grizzly. She stood as high as she could and set all her bristles on end; then, growling and chopping her teeth, she faced him.

The Grizzly, so far as I could see, took no notice of her. He came striding toward the feast as though alone. But when Grumpy got within twelve feet of him she uttered a succession of short, coughy roars, and, charging, gave

Then They Clinched.

him a tremendous blow on the ear. The Grizzly was surprised; but he replied with a left-hander that knocked her over like a sack of hay.

Nothing daunted, but doubly furious, she jumped up and rushed at him.

Then they clinched and rolled over and over, whacking and pounding, snorting and growling, and making no end of dust and rumpus. But above all their noise I could clearly hear Little Johnny, yelling at the top of his voice, and evidently encouraging his mother to go right in and finish the Grizzly at once.

Why the Grizzly did not break her in two I could not understand. After a few minutes' struggle, during which I could see nothing but dust and dim flying legs, the two separated as by mutual consent,—perhaps the regulation time was up,—and for a while they stood glaring at each other, Grumpy at least much winded.

The Grizzly would have dropped the matter right there. He did not wish to fight. He had no idea of troubling himself about Johnny. All he wanted was a quiet meal. But no! The moment he took one step toward the gar-

bage-pile, that is, as Grumpy thought, toward
Johnny, she went at him again. But this time
the Grizzly was ready for her. With one blow
he knocked her off her feet and sent her crashing on to a huge upturned pine-root. She was
fairly staggered this time. The force of the
blow, and the rude reception of the rooty antlers,
seemed to take all the fight out of her. She
scrambled over and tried to escape. But the
Grizzly was mad now. He meant to punish
her, and dashed around the root. For a minute
they kept up a dodging chase about it; but
Grumpy was quicker of foot, and somehow always managed to keep the root between herself
and her foe, while Johnny, safe in the tree,
continued to take an intense and uproarious
interest.

At length, seeing he could not catch her that
way, the Grizzly sat up on his haunches; and
while he doubtless was planning a new move,
old Grumpy saw her chance, and making a
dash, got away from the root and up to the top
of the tree where Johnny was perched.

Johnny came down a little way to meet her,
or perhaps so that the tree might not break off

## Johnny Bear

with the additional weight. Having photo-
graphed this interesting group from my hiding-
place, I thought I must get a closer picture at
any price, and for the first time in the day's pro-
ceedings I jumped out of the hole and ran under
the tree. This move proved a great mistake, for
here the thick lower boughs came between, and
I could see nothing at all of the Bears at the top.

I was close to the trunk, and was peering
about and seeking for a chance to use the
camera, when old Grumpy began to come down,
chopping her teeth and uttering her threatening
cough at me. While I stood in doubt, I heard
a voice far behind me calling:

"Say, Mister! You better look out; that ole
B'ar is liable to hurt you."

I turned to see the cow-boy of the Hotel on
his Horse. He had been riding after the cattle,
and chanced to pass near just as events were
moving quickly.

"Do you know these Bears?" said I, as he
rode up.

"Wall, I reckon I do," said he. "That there
little one up top is Johnny; he's a little crank.
An' the big un is Grumpy; she's a big crank.

## Johnny Bear

She's mighty onreliable gen'relly, but she's always strictly ugly when Johnny hollers like that."

"I should much like to get her picture when
she comes down," said I.

"Tell ye what I'll do: I'll stay by on the
pony, an' if she goes to bother you I reckon I
can keep her off," said the man.

He accordingly stood by as Grumpy slowly
came down from branch to branch, growling
and threatening. But when she neared the
ground she kept on the far side of the trunk,
and finally slipped down and ran into the woods,
without the slightest pretence of carrying out
any of her dreadful threats. Thus Johnny was
again left alone. He climbed up to his old
perch and resumed his monotonous whining:

*Wah! Wah! Wah!* ("Oh, dear! Oh, dear!
Oh, dear!")

I got the camera ready, and was arranging deliberately to take his picture in his favorite and
peculiar attitude for threnodic song, when all at
once he began craning his neck and yelling, as
he had done during the fight.

I looked where his nose pointed, and here
was the Grizzly coming on straight toward me

172

## Johnny Bear

—not charging, but striding along, as though he meant to come the whole distance.

I said to my cow-boy friend: " Do you know this Bear? "

He replied: " Wall! I reckon I do. That's the ole Grizzly. He's the biggest B'ar in the Park. He gen'relly minds his own business, but he ain't scared o' nothin'; an' to-day, ye see, he's been scrappin', so he's liable to be ugly."

" I would like to take his picture," said I; " and if you will help me, I am willing to take some chances on it."

" All right," said he, with a grin. " I'll stand by on the Horse, an' if he charges you I'll charge him; an' I kin knock him down once, but I can't do it twice. You better have your tree picked out."

As there was only one tree to pick out, and that was the one that Johnny was in, the prospect was not alluring. I imagined myself scrambling up there next to Johnny, and then Johnny's mother coming up after me, with the Grizzly below to catch me when Grumpy should throw me down.

# Johnny Bear

The Grizzly came on, and I snapped him at forty yards, then again at twenty yards; and still he came quietly toward me. I sat down on the garbage and made ready. Eighteen yards—sixteen yards—twelve yards—eight yards, and still he came, while the pitch of Johnny's protests kept rising proportionately. Finally at five yards he stopped, and swung his huge bearded head to one side, to see what was making that aggravating row in the tree-top, giving me a profile view, and I snapped the camera. At the click he turned on me with a thunderous

G—R—O—W—L!

and I sat still and trembling, wondering if my last moment had come. For a second he glared at me, and I could note the little green electric lamp in each of his eyes. Then he slowly turned and picked up—a large tomato-can.

"Goodness!" I thought, "is he going to throw that at me?" But he deliberately licked it out, dropped it, and took another, paying thenceforth no heed whatever either to me or to Johnny, evidently considering us equally beneath his notice.

174

# Johnny Bear

I backed slowly and respectfully out of his royal presence, leaving him in possession of the garbage, while Johnny kept on caterwauling from his safety-perch.

What became of Grumpy the rest of that day I do not know. Johnny, after bewailing for a time, realized that there was no sympathetic hearer of his cries, and therefore very sagaciously stopped them. Having no mother now to plan for him, he began to plan for himself, and at once proved that he was better stuff than he seemed. After watching, with a look of profound cunning on his little black face, and waiting till the Grizzly was some distance away, he silently slipped down behind the trunk, and, despite his three-leggedness, ran like a hare to the next tree, never stopping to breathe till he was on its topmost bough. For he was thoroughly convinced that the only object that the Grizzly had in life was to kill him, and he seemed quite aware that his enemy could not climb a tree.

Another long and safe survey of the Grizzly, who really paid no heed to him whatever, was followed by another dash for the next tree,

175

varied occasionally by a cunning feint to mislead the foe. So he went dashing from tree to
tree and climbing each to its very top, although
it might be but ten feet from the last, till
he disappeared in the woods. After, perhaps,
ten minutes, his voice again came floating
on the breeze, the habitual querulous whining which told me he had found his mother
and had resumed his customary appeal to her
sympathy.

## VI

It is quite a common thing for Bears to spank
their cubs when they need it, and if Grumpy
had disciplined Johnny this way, it would have
saved them both a deal of worry.

Perhaps not a day passed, that summer, without Grumpy getting into trouble on Johnny's
account. But of all these numerous occasions
the most ignominious was shortly after the af-
fair with the Grizzly.

I first heard the story from three bronzed
mountaineers. As they were very sensitive
about having their word doubted, and very
good shots with the revolver, I believed every

# Johnny Bear

word they told me, especially when afterward fully indorsed by the Park authorities.

It seemed that of all the tinned goods on the pile the nearest to Johnny's taste were marked with a large purple plum. This conclusion he had arrived at only after most exhaustive study. The very odor of those plums in Johnny's nostrils was the equivalent of ecstasy. So when it came about one day that the cook of the Hotel baked a huge batch of plum-tarts, the telltale wind took the story afar into the woods, where it was wafted by way of Johnny's nostrils to his very soul.

Of course Johnny was whimpering at the time. His mother was busy "washing his face and combing his hair," so he had double cause for whimpering. But the smell of the tarts thrilled him; he jumped up, and when his mother tried to hold him he squalled, and I am afraid—he bit her. She should have cuffed him, but she did not. She only gave a disapproving growl, and followed to see that he came to no harm.

With his little black nose in the wind, Johnny led straight for the kitchen. He took the

177

precaution, however, of climbing from time to time to the very top of a pine-tree lookout to take an observation, while Grumpy stayed below.

Thus they came close to the kitchen, and there, in the last tree, Johnny's courage as a leader gave out, so he remained aloft and expressed his hankering for tarts in a woe-begone wail.

It is not likely that Grumpy knew exactly what her son was crying for. But it is sure that as soon as she showed an inclination to go back into the pines, Johnny protested in such an outrageous and heartrending screeching that his mother simply could not leave him, and he showed no sign of coming down to be led away.

Grumpy herself was fond of plum-jam. The odor was now, of course, very strong and proportionately alluring; so Grumpy followed it somewhat cautiously up to the kitchen door.

There was nothing surprising about this. The rule of " live and let live " is so strictly enforced in the Park that the Bears often come to the kitchen door for pickings, and on getting something, they go quietly back to the woods.

178

# Johnny Bear

Doubtless Johnny and Grumpy would each have gotten their tart but that a new factor appeared in the case.

That week the Hotel people had brought a new Cat from the East. She was not much more than a kitten, but still had a litter of her own, and at the moment that Grumpy reached the door, the Cat and her family were sunning themselves on the top step. Pussy opened her eyes to see this huge, shaggy monster towering above her.

The Cat had never before seen a Bear—she had not been there long enough; she did not know even what a Bear was. She knew what a Dog was, and here was a bigger, more awful bobtailed black dog than ever she had dreamed of coming right at her. Her first thought was to fly for her life. But her next was for the kittens. She must take care of them. She must at least cover their retreat. So, like a brave little mother, she braced herself on that door-step, and spreading her back, her claws, her tail, and everything she had to spread, she screamed out at that Bear an unmistakable order to

STOP!

## Johnny Bear

The language must have been "Cat," but the meaning was clear to the Bear; for those who saw it maintain stoutly that Grumpy not only stopped, but she also conformed to the custom of the country and in token of surrender held up her hands.

However, the position she thus took made her so high that the Cat seemed tiny in the distance below. Old Grumpy had faced a Grizzly once, and was she now to be held up by a miserable little spike-tailed skunk no bigger than a mouthful? She was ashamed of herself, especially when a wail from Johnny smote on her ear and reminded her of her plain duty, as well as supplied his usual moral support.

So she dropped down on her front feet to proceed.

Again the Cat shrieked, "STOP!"

But Grumpy ignored the command. A scared mew from a kitten nerved the Cat, and she launched her ultimatum, which ultimatum was herself. Eighteen sharp claws, a mouthful of keen teeth, had Pussy, and she worked them all with a desperate will when she landed on Grumpy's bare, bald, sensitive nose, just the

180

" Stop ! " Shrieked the Cat.

spot of all where the Bear could not stand it, and then worked backward to a point outside the sweep of Grumpy's claws. After one or two vain attempts to shake the spotted fury off, old Grumpy did just as most creatures would have done under the circumstances: she turned tail and bolted out of the enemy's country into her own woods.

But Puss's fighting blood was up. She was not content with repelling the enemy; she wanted to inflict a crushing defeat, to achieve an absolute and final rout. And however fast old Grumpy might go, it did not count, for the Cat was still on top, working her teeth and claws like a little demon. Grumpy, always erratic, now became panic-stricken. The trail of the pair was flecked with tufts of long black hair, and there was even bloodshed (in the fiftieth degree). Honor surely was satisfied, but Pussy was not. Round and round they had gone in the mad race. Grumpy was frantic, absolutely humiliated, and ready to make any terms; but Pussy seemed deaf to her cough-like yelps, and no one knows how far the Cat might have ridden that day had not Johnny unwittingly

put a new idea into his mother's head by bawl-
ing in his best style from the top of his last
tree, which tree Grumpy made for and scrambled up.

This was so clearly the enemy's country and
in view of his reinforcements that the Cat wisely
decided to follow no farther.   She jumped
from the climbing Bear to the ground, and
then mounted sentry-guard below, marching
around with tail in the air, daring that Bear to
come down.   Then the kittens came out and
sat around, and enjoyed it all hugely.   And the
mountaineers assured me that the Bears would
have been kept up the tree till they were starved,
had not the cook of the Hotel come out and
called off his Cat—although this statement was
not among those vouched for by the officers of
the Park.

## VII

THE last time I saw Johnny he was in the top
of a tree, bewailing his unhappy lot as usual,
while his mother was dashing about among the
pines, "with a chip on her shoulder," seeking
for some one—any one—that she could punish

Then Pussy Launched her Ultimatum.

for Johnny's sake, provided, of course, that it was not a big Grizzly or a Mother Cat.

This was early in August, but there were not lacking symptoms of change in old Grumpy. She was always reckoned "onsartain," and her devotion to Johnny seemed subject to her characteristic. This perhaps accounted for the fact that when the end of the month was near, Johnny would sometimes spend half a day in the top of some tree, alone, miserable, and utterly unheeded.

The last chapter of his history came to pass after I had left the region. One day at gray dawn he was tagging along behind his mother as she prowled in the rear of the Hotel. A newly hired Irish girl was already astir in the kitchen. On looking out, she saw, as she thought, a Calf where it should not be, and ran to shoo it away. That open kitchen door still held unmeasured terrors for Grumpy, and she ran in such alarm that Johnny caught the infection, and not being able to keep up with her, he made for the nearest tree, which unfortunately turned out to be a post, and soon—too soon— he arrived at its top, some seven feet from the ground, and there poured forth his woes on the

187

chilly morning air, while Grumpy apparently felt justified in continuing her flight alone. When the girl came near and saw that she had treed some wild animal, she was as much frightened as her victim. But others of the kitchen staff appeared, and recognizing the vociferous Johnny, they decided to make him a prisoner.

A collar and chain were brought, and after a struggle, during which several of the men got well scratched, the collar was buckled on Johnny's neck and the chain made fast to the post.

When he found that he was held, Johnny was simply too mad to scream. He bit and scratched and tore till he was tired out. Then he lifted up his voice again to call his mother. She did appear once or twice in the distance, but could not make up her mind to face that Cat, so disappeared, and Johnny was left to his fate.

He put in the most of that day in alternate struggling and crying. Toward evening he was worn out, and glad to accept the meal that was brought by Norah, who felt herself called on to play mother, since she had chased his own mother away.

When night came it was very cold; but

188

## Johnny Bear

Johnny nearly froze at the top of the post before he would come down and accept the warm
bed provided at the bottom.

During the days that followed, Grumpy
came often to the garbage-heap, but soon
apparently succeeded in forgetting all about her
son. He was daily tended by Norah, and received all his meals from her. He also received
something else; for one day he scratched her
when she brought his food, and she very properly spanked him till he squealed. For a few
hours he sulked; he was not used to such
treatment. But hunger subdued him, and
thenceforth he held his new guardian in whole-
some respect. She, too, began to take an interest in the poor motherless little wretch, and
within a fortnight Johnny showed signs of de-
veloping a new character. He was much less
noisy. He still expressed his hunger in a whining *Er-r-r Er-r-r Er-r-r,* but he rarely squealed
now, and his unruly outbursts entirely ceased.

By the third week of September the change
was still more marked. Utterly abandoned by
his own mother, all his interest had centred in
Norah, and she had fed and spanked him into

189

an exceedingly well-behaved little Bear. Sometimes she would allow him a taste of freedom,
and he then showed his bias by making, not for
the woods, but for the kitchen where she was,
and following her around on his hind legs.
Here also he made the acquaintance of that
dreadful Cat; but Johnny had a powerful friend
now, and Pussy finally became reconciled to
the black, woolly interloper.

As the Hotel was to be closed in October,
there was talk of turning Johnny loose or of
sending him to the Washington Zoo; but Norah
had claims that she would not forego.

When the frosty nights of late September
came, Johnny had greatly improved in his man-
ners, but he had also developed a bad cough.
An examination of his lame leg had shown that
the weakness was not in the foot, but much
more deeply seated, perhaps in the hip, and that
meant a feeble and tottering constitution.

He did not get fat, as do most Bears in fall;
indeed, he continued to fail. His little round
belly shrank in, his cough became worse, and
one morning he was found very sick and shiver-
ing in his bed by the post. Norah brought

190

him indoors, where the warmth helped him so much that thenceforth he lived in the kitchen.

For a few days he seemed better, and his old-time pleasure in *seeing things* revived. The great blazing fire in the range particularly appealed to him, and made him sit up in his old attitude when the opening of the door brought the wonder to view. After a week he lost interest even in that, and drooped more and more each day. Finally not the most exciting noises or scenes around him could stir up his old fondness for seeing what was going on.

He coughed a good deal, too, and seemed wretched, except when in Norah's lap. Here he would cuddle up contentedly, and whine most miserably when she had to set him down again in his basket.

A few days before the closing of the Hotel, he refused his usual breakfast, and whined softly till Norah took him in her lap; then he feebly snuggled up to her, and his soft *Er-r-r Er-r-r* grew fainter, till it ceased. Half an hour later, when she laid him down to go about her work, Little Johnny had lost the last trace of his anxiety to see and know what was going on.

N

# The Mother Teal and the
# Overland Route

# The Mother Teal and the Overland Route

## I

 GREEN–WINGED Teal had made her nest in the sedge by one of the grass-edged pools that fleck the sunny slope of the Riding Mountain.   The passing half-breed,   driving   his creaking ox-wagon, saw only a pond with the usual fringe of coarse grass, beyond which was a belt of willow scrub and an old poplar-tree.   But the little Teal in the rushes, and her neighbors, the Flickers, on the near-by poplar, saw in the nestling pool a kingdom, a perfect paradise, for this was home.   Now was the ripeness of the love-moon, with the mother-moon at hand in its

fulness of promise. Indeed, the little Flickers had almost chipped their glassy shells, and the eggs, the ten treasures of the Teal, had lost the look of mere interesting things, and were putting on, each, an air of sleeping personality, warm, sentient, pulsatory, and almost vocal.

The little Teal had lost her mate early in the season. At least, he had disappeared, and as the land abounded in deadly foes, it was fair to suppose him dead. But her attention was fully taken up with her nest and her brood.

All through the latter part of June she tended them carefully, leaving but a little while each day to seek food, and then covering them carefully with a dummy foster-mother that she had made of down from her own breast.

One morning, as she flew away, leaving the dummy in charge, she heard an ominous crackling in the thick willows near at hand, but she wisely went on. When she returned, her neighbor, the Flicker, was still uttering a note of alarm, and down by her own nest were the fresh tracks of a man. The dummy mother had been disturbed, but, strange to tell, the eggs were all there and unharmed.

196

# The Mother Teal and the Overland Route

The enemy, though so near, had been baffled after all. As the days went by, and the grand finish of her task drew near, the little Green-wing felt the mother-love growing in her heart to be ready for the ten little prisoners that her devotion was to set free. They were no longer mere eggs, she felt, and sometimes she would talk to them in low raucous tones, and they would seem to answer from within in whispered "peepings," or perhaps in sounds that have no human name because too fine for human ear. So there is small wonder that when they do come out they have already learned many of the few simple words that make up Teal-talk.

The many hazards of the early nesting-time were rapidly passed, but a new one came. The growing springtime had turned into a drought. No rain had fallen for many, many days, and as the greatest day of all drew near, the mother saw with dismay that the pond was shrinking, quickly shrinking. Already it was rimmed about by a great stretch of bare mud, and unless the rains came soon, the first experience of the little ones would be a perilous overland journey.

197

## The Mother Teal and the Overland Route

It was just as impossible to hurry up the hatching as it was to bring rain, and the last few days of the mother's task were, as she had feared, in view of a wide mud-flat where once had been the pond.

They all came out at last. The little china tombs were broken one by one, disclosing each a little Teal: ten little balls of mottled down, ten little cushions of yellow plush, ten little golden caskets with jewel eyes, enshrining each a priceless spark of life.

But fate had been so harsh. It was now a matter of life and death to reach a pond. Oh, why did not Old Sol give the downlings three days of paddling to strengthen on before enforcing this dreadful journey overland? The mother must face the problem and face it now, or lose them all.

The Ducklings do not need to eat for several hours after they are hatched. Their bodies are yet sustained by the provender of their last abode. But once that is used they must eat. The nearest pond was half a mile away. And the great questions were: Can these baby Ducks hold out that long? Can they escape the countless dangers of the road? For not a

## The Mother Teal and the Overland Route

Harrier, Falcon, Hawk, Fox, Weasel, Coyote,
Gopher, Ground-squirrel, or Snake but would
count them his lawful prey.

All this the mother felt instinctively, even if
she did not set it forth in clear expression ; and
as soon as the ten were warmed and lively she
led them into the grass. Such a scrambling
and peeping and tumbling about as they tried to
get through and over the grass-stalks that, like a
bamboo forest, barred their way! Their mother
had to watch the ten with one eye and the whole
world with the other, for not a friend had she
or they outside of themselves. The countless
living things about were either foes or neutral.

## II

AFTER a long scramble through the grass they
climbed a bank and got among the poplar
scrub, and here sat down to rest. One little
fellow that had struggled along bravely with
the others was so weak that there seemed no
chance of his reaching that far-away Happy-
land, the pond.

When they were rested, their mother gave a

## The Mother Teal and the Overland Route

low, gentle *quack* that doubtless meant, " Come
along, children," and they set off again, scrambling over and around the twigs, each peeping
softly when he was getting along nicely, or
plaintively when he found himself caught in
some thicket.

At last they came to a wide open place.   It
was easy to travel here, but there was great
danger of Hawks.   The mother rested long in
the edge of the thicket, and scanned the sky in
every direction before she ventured into the
open.   Then, when all was clear, she marshalled
her little army for a dash over this great desert
of nearly one hundred yards.

The little fellows bravely struggled after her,
their small yellow bodies raised at an angle,
and their tiny wings held out like arms as they
pushed along after " mother."

She was anxious to finish it all at one dash,
but soon saw that that was hopeless.   The
strongest of her brood could keep up with her,
but the others dragged in order of weakness.
The brood now formed a little procession over
twenty feet long, and the weakling was nearly
ten feet behind that again.

## The Mother Teal and the Overland Route

A dangerous rest in the open was now enforced. The peepers came panting up to their mother, and full of anxiety, she lay there beside them till they were able to go on. Then she led them as before, quacking gently, " Courage, my darlings!"

They were not half-way to the pond yet, and the journey was telling on them long before they reached this last friendly thicket. The brood strung out into another procession, with a wide gap to the runtie in the rear, when a great Marsh Hawk suddenly appeared skimming low over the ground.

"Squat!" gasped Mother Greenwing, and the little things all lay flat, except the last one. Too far off to hear the low warning, he struggled on. The great Hawk swooped, seized him in his claws, and bore him peeping away over the bushes. All the poor mother could do was gaze in dumb sorrow as the bloodthirsty pirate bore off the downling, unresisted and unpunished. Yet, no; not entirely; for, as he flew straight to the bank of the pond where lodged his crew of young marauders, he heedlessly passed over the home bush of a

## The Mother Teal and the Overland Route

Kingbird, and that fearless little warrior screamed out his battle-cry as he launched in air to give chase. Away went the pirate, and away went the King, the one huge, heavy, and cowardly, the other small, swift, and fearless as a hero, away and away, out of sight, the Kingbird gaining at every stroke, till his voice was lost in the distance.

The sorrow of the Mother Greenwing, if less deep than that of the human mother, was yet very real. But she had now the nine to guard. They needed her every thought. She led them as quickly as possible into the bushes, and for a time they breathed more freely.

Thenceforth she managed to have the journey lie through the cover. An hour or more passed by in slight alarms and in many rests, and the pond was very near; and well it was, for the Ducklings were almost worn out, their little paddles were scratched and bleeding, and their strength was all but gone. For a time they gasped under shadow of the last tall bush before again setting out in a compact flock to cross the next bare place, a rough opening through the poplars.

## The Mother Teal and the Overland Route

And they never knew that death in another form had hovered on their track. A Red Fox crossed the trail of the little Duck army. His keen nose told him at once that here was a feast awaiting, and all he had to do was follow it up and eat. So he sneaked softly and swiftly along their well-marked trail. He was already in sight of them. In the ordinary course he soon would have them, mother and all, but the ordinary course may go askew. He was near enough to count the little marchers, if count he could, when the wind brought something which made him stop, crouch low, then, at a surer whiff, he slunk away, fled as swiftly as he could without being seen. And the realest danger, surest death of all that had threatened, was thwarted by an unseen power, and not even the watchful Mother Duck had the slightest hint of it.

### III

THE little ones now toddled along after their mother, who led them quickly to cross the opening. To her delight, a long arm of the pond was quite close, just across that treeless

lane. She made straight for it, joyfully calling,
" Come, my darlings! "

But alas! the treeless opening was one of
the man-made things called a " cart-trail." On
each side of it were two deep-worn, endless cañons
that man calls " wheel-ruts," and into the first of
these fell four of her brood. Five managed to
scramble across, but the other rut was yet deeper
and wider, and the five were there engulfed.

Oh, dear, this was terrible! The little ones
were too weak now to climb out. The ruts
seemed endless in both directions, and the
mother did not know how to help them. She
and they were in despair, and as she ran about
calling and urging them to put forth all their
strength, there came up suddenly the very
thing she most feared,—the deadliest enemy of
Ducks,—a great tall man.

Mother Greenwing flung herself at his feet
and flopped on the grass. Not begging for
mercy! Oh, no! She was only trying to trick
the man into thinking she was wounded, so that
he would follow her, and she could lead him
away.

But this man knew the trick, and he would

## The Mother Teal and the Overland Route

not follow. Instead of that he looked about,
and found the nine little bright-eyed downlings deep in the ruts, vainly trying to hide.

He stooped gently, and gathered them all
into his hat. Poor little things, how they did
*peep!* Poor little mother, how she did cry
in bitterness for her brood! Now she knew
that they all were to be destroyed before her
very eyes, and she beat her breast on the
ground before the terrible giant in agony of
sorrow.

Then the heartless monster went to the edge
of the pond, no doubt for a drink to wash the
Ducklings down his throat. He bent down,
and a moment later the Ducklings were spat-
tering free over the water. The mother flew out
on the glassy surface. She called, and they all
came skurrying to her. She did not know that
this man was really her friend; she never knew
that he was the divinity whose mere presence
had been enough to drive the Fox away and
to save them in their direst strait,—his race has
persecuted hers too long,—and she went on
hating him to the end.

She tried to lead her brood far away from

## The Mother Teal and the Overland Route

him. She took them right across the open pond. This was a mistake, for it exposed them to other, to real, enemies. That great Marsh Hawk saw them, and he came swooping along, sure of getting one in each claw.

"Run for the rushes!" called out the Mother Greenwing; and run they all did, pattering over the surface as fast as their tired little legs could go.

"Run! run!" cried the mother. But the Hawk was close at hand now. In spite of all their running he would be upon them in another second. They were too young to dive. There seemed no escape, when, just as he pounced, the bright little mother gave a great splash with all her strength, and using both feet and wings, dashed the water all over the Hawk. He was astonished. He sprang back into the air to shake himself dry. The mother urged the little ones to "keep on." Keep on they did. But down came the Hawk again, again to be repelled with a shower of spray. Three times did he pounce, three times did she drench him, till at last all the downlings were safe in the friendly rushes. The angry Hawk now made a

206

Three Times Did She Drench Him.

O

## The Mother Teal and the Overland Route

lunge at the mother; but she could dive, and giving a good-by splash, she easily disappeared.

Far in the rushes she came up, and called a gentle *quack, quack!* The nine tired little ones came to her, and safely they rested at last.

But that was not all. Just as they began to feast on the teeming insect life, a far-away faint peep was heard. Mother Greenwing called again her mothering *qu-a-a-a-a-a-c-c—k.* And through the sedge demurely paddling, like an old-timer, came their missing one that the Hawk had carried off.

He had not been hurt by the claws. The valiant Kingbird had overtaken the Hawk over the pond. At the first blow of his bill the Hawk had shrieked and dropped his prey; the little Duck fell unharmed into the water, and escaped into the rushes till his mother and brothers came, then he rejoined them, and they lived happily in the great pond till they all grew up and flew away on wings of their own.

# Chink: The Development of a Pup

# Chink: The Development
of a Pup

## I

CHINK was just old enough to think himself a very re-markable little Dog; and so he was, but not in the way he fondly imagined. He was neither fierce nor dreadful, strong nor swift, but he was one of the noisiest, best-natured, silliest Pups that ever chewed his master's boots to bits.  His master, Bill Aubrey, was an old mountaineer who was camped below Garnet Peak in the Yellowstone Park.  This is in a very quiet corner, far from the usual line of travel, and Bill's camp, before ours came, would have been a very lonely place but for his com-

panion, this irrepressible, woolly-coated little Dog.

Chink was never still for five minutes. Indeed, he would do anything he was told to do except keep still. He was always trying to do some absurd and impossible thing, or, if he did attempt the possible, he usually spoiled his best effort by his way of going about it. He once spent a whole morning trying to run up a tall, straight pine-tree in whose branches was a snickering Pine Squirrel.

The darling ambition of his life for some weeks was to catch one of the Picket-pin Gophers that swarmed on the prairie about the camp. These little animals have a trick of sitting bolt upright on their hind legs, with their paws held close in, so that at a distance they look exactly like picket-pins. Often when we went out to picket our horses for the night we would go toward a Gopher, thinking it was a picket-pin already driven in, and would find out the mistake only when it dived into the ground with a defiant chirrup.

Chink had determined to catch one of these Gophers the very first day he came into the valley. Of course he went about it in his own original way, doing everything wrong end first, as usual. This, his master said, was due to a streak of Irish in his make-up. So Chink would begin a most elaborate stalk a quarter of a mile from the Gopher. After crawling on his breast from tussock to tussock for a hundred yards or so, the nervous strain became too great, and Chink, getting too much excited to crawl, would rise on his feet and walk straight toward the Gopher, which would now be sitting up by its hole, fully alive to the situation.

After a minute or two of this very open approach, Chink's excitement would overpower all caution. He would begin running, and at the last, just as he should have done his finest stalking, he would go bounding and barking toward the Gopher, which would sit like a peg of wood till the proper moment, then dive below with a derisive chirrup, throwing with its hind feet a lot of sand right into Chink's eager, open mouth.

Day after day this went on with level sameness, and still Chink did not give up. Perseverance, he seemed to believe, must surely

win in the end, as indeed it did. For one day he made an unusually elaborate stalk after an unusually fine Gopher, carried out all his absurd tactics, finishing with the grand, boisterous charge, and actually caught his victim; but this time it happened to be a wooden picket-pin. Any one who doubts that a Dog knows when he has made a fool of himself should have seen Chink that day as he sheepishly sneaked out of sight behind the tent.

But failure had no lasting effect on Chink. There was a streak of grit as well as Irish in him that carried him through every reverse, and nothing could dash his good nature. He was into everything with the maximum of energy and the minimum of discretion, delighted as long as he could be always up and doing.

Every passing wagon and horseman and grazing Calf had to be chivvied, and if the Cat from the guard-house strayed by, Chink felt that it was a solemn duty he owed to the soldiers, the Cat, and himself to chase her home at frightful speed. He would dash twenty times a day after an old hat that Bill used deliberately to throw into a Wasps' nest with the order, " Fetch it!"

It took time, but countless disasters began to tell. Chink slowly realized that there were long whips and big, fierce Dogs with wagons; that Horses have teeth in their heels; that Calves have relatives with clubs on their heads; that a slow Cat may turn out a Skunk; and that Wasps are not Butterflies. Yes, it took an uncommonly long time, but it all told in the end. Chink began to develop a grain—a little one, but a living, growing grain—of good Dog sense.

## II

It seemed as if all his blunders were the rough, unsymmetrical stones of an arch, and the keystone was added, the structure, his character, made strong and complete, by his crowning blunder in the matter of a large Coyote.

This Coyote lived not far from our camp, and he evidently realized, as all the animals there do, that no man is allowed to shoot, trap, hunt, or in any way molest the wild creatures in the Park; above all, in this part, close to the

military patrol, with soldiers always on watch. Secure in the knowledge of this, the Coyote used to come about the camp each night for scraps. At first I found only his tracks in the dust, as though he had circled the camp but feared to come very near. Then we began to hear his weird evening song just after sundown, or about sun-up. At length his track was plain in the dust about the scrap-bucket each morning when I went out to learn from the trail what animals had been there during the night. Then growing bolder, he came about the camp occasionally in the daytime. Shyly at first, but with increasing assurance, as he was satisfied of his immunity, until finally he was not only there every night, but seemed to hang around nearly all day, sneaking in to steal whatever was eatable, or sitting in plain view on some rising ground at a distance.

One morning, as he sat on a bank some fifty yards away, one of us, in a spirit of mischief, said to Chink: " Chink, do you see that Coyote over there grinning at you? Go and chase him out of that."

Chink always did as he was told, and burning

to distinguish himself, he dashed after the Coyote, who loped lightly away, and there was a pretty good race for a quarter of a mile; but it was nothing to the race which began when the Coyote turned on his pursuer.

Chink realized all at once that he had been lured into the power of a Tartar, and strained every muscle to get back to camp. The Coyote was swifter, and soon overtook the Dog, nipping him first on one side, then on the other, with manifest glee, as if he were cracking a series of good jokes at Chink's expense.

Chink yelped and howled and ran his hardest, but had no respite from his tormentor till he dashed right into camp; and we, I am afraid, laughed with the Coyote, and the Puppy did not get the sympathy he deserved for his trouble in doing as he was told.

One more experience like this, on a smaller scale, was enough to dampen even Chink's enthusiasm. He decided to let that Coyote very much alone in future.

Not so the Coyote, however. He had discovered a new and delightful amusement. He came daily now and hung about the camp,

Chink: The Development of a Pup

knowing perfectly well that no one would dare
to shoot him.   Indeed, the lock of every gun
in the party was sealed up by the government
officials, and soldiers were everywhere on watch
to enforce the laws.

Thenceforth that Coyote lay in wait for poor
Chink, and sought every opportunity to tease
him.   The little Dog learned that if he went
a hundred yards from camp alone, the Coyote
would go after him, and bite and chase him
right back to his master's tent.

Day after day this went on, until at last
Chink's life was made a misery to him.   He
did not dare now to go fifty yards from the
tent alone ; and even if he went with us when
we rode, that fierce and impudent Coyote was
sure to turn up and come along, trotting close
beside or behind, watching for a chance to
worry poor Chink and spoiling all his pleasure
in the ramble, but keeping just out of reach of
our quirts, or a little farther off when we stopped
to pick up some stones.

One day Aubrey moved his camp a mile up-
stream, and we saw less of the Coyote, for the
reason that he moved a mile up-stream too,

## Chink: The Development of a Pup

and, like all bullies who are unopposed, grew more insolent and tyrannical every day, until poor little Chink's life became at last a veritable reign of terror, at which his master merely laughed.

Aubrey gave it out that he had moved camp to get better Horse-feed. It soon turned out, however, that he wanted to be alone while he enjoyed the contents of a whiskey-flask that he had obtained somewhere. But one flask was a mere starter for him. The second day he mounted his Horse, said, "Chink, you watch the tent," and rode away over the mountains to the nearest saloon, leaving Chink obediently curled up on some sacking.

### III

Now, with all his puppyish silliness, Chink was a faithful watch-dog, and his master knew that he would take care of the tent as well as he could.

Late that afternoon a passing mountaineer came along. When he was within shouting distance he stopped, as is customary, and shouted:

## Chink: The Development of a Pup

" Hello there, Bill!  Oh, Bill!"

But getting no answer, he went up to the door, and there was met by " an odd-looking Purp with his bristles all on end "; and Chink, for of course it was he, warned him in many fierce growls to keep away.

The mountaineer understood the situation and went on.  Evening came, and no master to relieve Chink, who was now getting very hungry.

There was some bacon in the tent wrapped in a bag, but that was sacred.  His master had told him to " watch it," and Chink would have starved rather than touch it.

He ventured out on the flat in hope of finding a mouse or something to stay the pangs of hunger, when suddenly he was pounced on by that brute of a Coyote, and the old chase was repeated as Chink dashed back to the tent.

There a change came over him.  The remembrance of his duty seemed suddenly to alter him and brace him up, just as the cry of her Kitten will turn a timid Cat into a Tigress.

He was a mere Puppy yet, and a little fool

in many ways, but away back of all was a fibre of strength that would grow with his years. The moment that Coyote tried to follow into the tent,—his master's tent,—Chink forgot all his own fears, and turned on the enemy like a little demon.

The beasts feel the force of right and wrong They know moral courage and cowardice. The moral force was all with the little scared Dog, and both animals seemed to know it. The Coyote backed off, growling savagely, and vowing, in Coyote fashion, to tear that Dog to ribbons very soon. All the same, he did not venture to enter the tent, as he clearly had intended doing.

Then began a literal siege; for the Coyote came back every little while, and walked round the tent, scratching contemptuously with his hind feet, or marching up to the open door, to be met at once, face to face, by poor little Chink, who, really half dead with fear, was brave again as soon as he saw any attempt to injure the things in his charge.

All this time Chink had nothing to eat. He could slip out and get a drink at the near-by

223

P

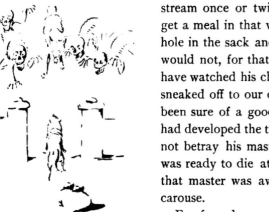

stream once or twice a day, but he could not get a meal in that way. He could have torn a hole in the sack and eaten some bacon, but he would not, for that was in trust; or he could have watched his chance to desert his post, and sneaked off to our camp, where he would have been sure of a good meal. But no; adversity had developed the true Dog in him. He would not betray his master's trust in any way. He was ready to die at his post, if need be, while that master was away indulging in a drunken carouse.

For four days and four nights of misery did this heroic little Dog keep his place, and keep tent and stuff from the Coyote that he held in mortal terror.

On the fifth morning old Aubrey had awakened to the fact that he was not at home, and that his camp in the mountains was guarded only by a small Dog. He was tired of his spree now, and he got on his Horse and set out over the hills, sober but very shaky. When he was about half-way on the trail it suddenly dawned on his clouded brain that he had left Chink without any food.

Trembling with Fear and Weakness, He was
Making his Last Stand.

# Chink: The Development of a Pup

"Hope the little beast hain't spoiled all my bacon," he thought, and he pressed on more briskly till he came to the ridge commanding a view of his tent. There it was, and there at the door, exchanging growls and snapping at each other, were the big, fierce Coyote and poor little Chink.

"Wal, I be darned!" exclaimed Aubrey. "I forgot all about that blasted Coyote. Poor Chink! he must 'a' had a mighty tough time. Wonder he ain't all chawed up an' the camp in tatters."

There he was, bravely making his last stand. His legs were tottering under him with fear and hunger, but he still put on his boldest face, and was clearly as ready as ever to die in defence of the camp.

The cold gray eyes of the mountaineer took in this part of the situation at the first glance, and when he galloped up and saw the untouched bacon, he realized that Chink had eaten nothing since he left. When the Puppy, trembling with fear and weakness, crawled up and looked in his face and licked his hand as much as to say, "I've done what you told me,"

227

## Chink: The Development of a Pup

it was too much for old Aubrey. The tears
stood in his eyes as he hastened to get food for
the little hero.

Then he turned to him and said: " Chink,
old pard, I've treated you dirty, an' you always
treated me white. I'll never go on another
spree without takin' you along, Chink, an' I'll
treat you as white as you treated me, if I know
how. 'Tain't much more I kin do for you, pard,
since ye don't drink, but I reckon I kin lift the
biggest worry out o' yer life, an' I'll do it, too."

Then from the ridge-pole he took down the
pride of his heart, his treasured repeating rifle,
and, regardless of consequences, he broke the
government seals, wax eagles, red tape, and all,
and went to the door.

The Coyote was sitting off a little way with a
Mephistophelian grin on his face, as usual; but
the rifle rang, and Chink's reign of terror was
at an end.

WHAT matter if the soldiers did come out and
find that the laws of the Park had been violated,
that Aubrey had shot one of the animals of the
Park?

## Chink: The Development of a Pup

What matter to Aubrey if his gun was taken from him and destroyed, and he and his outfit expelled from the Park, with a promise of being jailed if ever he returned? What did it all matter?

"It's all right," said old Aubrey. "I done the squar' thing by my pard—my pard, that always treated me white."

The Kangaroo Rat

# The Kangaroo Rat

## I

T was a rough, rock-built, squalid ranch-house that I lived in, on the Currumpaw. The plaster of the walls was mud, the roof and walls were dry mud, the great river-flat around it was sandy mud, and the hills a mile away were piled-up mud, sculptured by frost and rain into the oddest of mud vagaries, with here and there a coping of lava to prevent the utter demolition of some necessary mud pinnacle by the indefatigable sculptors named.

The place seemed uninviting to a stranger from the lush and fertile prairies of Manitoba, but the more I saw of it the more it was revealed

233

## The Kangaroo Rat

a paradise. For every cottonwood of the straggling belt that the river used to mark its doubtful
course across the plain, and every dwarfed and
spiny bush and weedy copse, was teeming with
*life*. And every day and every night I made
new friends, or learned new facts about the
mudland denizens.

Man and the Birds are understood to possess
the earth during the daylight, therefore the night
has become the time for the four-footed ones to
be about, and in order that I might set a sleep-
less watch on their movements I was careful
each night before going to bed to sweep smooth
the dust about the shanty and along the two pathways, one to the spring and one to the corral by
way of the former corn-patch, still called the
" garden."

Each morning I went out with all the feelings of a child meeting the Christmas postman,
or of a fisherman hauling in his largest net,
eager to know what there was for me.

Not a morning passed without a message
from the beasts. Nearly every night a Skunk
or two would come and gather up table-scraps,
prying into all sorts of forbidden places in their

# The Kangaroo Rat

search.  Once or twice a Bobcat came.  And one morning the faithful dust reported in grate detail how the Bobcat and the Skunk had differed.  There was evidence, too, that the Bobcat quickly said (in Bobcat, of course), " I beg pardon, I mistook you for a rabbit, but will never again make such a mistake."

More than once the sinister trail of the "Hydrophoby-cat" was recorded.  And on one occasion the great broad track of the King Wolf of the region came right up the pathway, nearly to the door, the tracks getting closer together as he neared it.  Then stopping, he had exactly retraced his steps and gone elsewhere about his business.  Jack-rabbits, Coyotes, and Cotton-tails all passed, and wrote for me a few original lines commemorative of their visit—and all were faithfully delivered on call next morning.

But always over and through all other tracks was a curious, delicate, lace-like fabric of polka-dots and interwoven sinuous lines.  It was there each morning, fresh made the night before, whatever else was missing.  But there was so much of its pattern that it was impossible to take any one line and follow it up.

# The Kangaroo Rat

At first it seemed to be made up of the trails of many small bipeds, each closely followed by its little one.   Now, man and Birds are the only bipeds, but these were clearly not the tracks of any Bird.   Trying to be judicial, I put together all the facts that the dust reported.   First, here was proof that a number of tiny, two-legged, fur-slippered creatures came nightly to dance in the moonlight.   Each one, as he pirouetted about, was closely followed by a much smaller one of the same kind, as though by his page. They came from nowhere and went again as they would.   And they must have been invisible at will, or else how escape the ever-watchful Coyotes?

If only this had been in England or Ireland, any peasant could have explained it offhand— invisible pairs of tiny, furry boots, dancing in the moonlight—why, the veriest idiot knows that—*fairies*, of course.

But in New Mexico I had never heard of such a thing.   In no work on this country, so far as I knew, was there any mention of their occurrence.

If only it could be!   Would it not be delight-

They Came Nightly to Dance in the Moonlight.

## The Kangaroo Rat

ful? I would gladly have believed. Christian Andersen would have insisted on believing in it, and then made others believe it, too. But for me, alas! it was impossible, for long ago, when my soul came to the fork in the trail marked on the left "To Arcadie," on the right "To Scientia," I took the flinty, upland right-hand path. I had given up my fayland eyes for—for I do not know what. And so I was puzzled, but the more puzzled, the more interested, of course; and remembering, from former experience, that it pays to offer a great deal of clear writing-space to the visitors who nightly favored me with their autographs, I made with unusual care a large extension of the clean-swept dust sheet, to which the sage-brush-scented evening wind added a still smoother finish, and which next day enabled me to follow out a single line of the point-lace pattern.

It went dimpling down the path, toward the six old corn-stumps called the garden, and then, leaving the clear written dust, it had turned aside, and seemed to end at a weed-covered mound, about which were several small holes that went in, not downward, but at a level.

239

Q

# The Kangaroo Rat

(Yes, of course, another pretty mystery nearly  gone. How sharp the flints are on this upland path!) I set a trap by these holes, and next morning I had surely caught my " fairy." Just the loveliest, daintiest fawn-brown little creature that ever was seen in fur: large beautiful eyes like a Fawn's—no, not like a Fawn's, for no Fawn that ever lived had such wonderfully innocent orbs of liquid brown, ears like thinnest shells of the sea, showing the pink veins' flood of life. His hind feet were large and strong; but his fore feet—his hands, I mean—were the tiniest of the tiny, pinky white and rounded and dimpled, just like a baby's, only whiter and smaller than the tip of baby's smallest finger. His throat and breast were snowy white. However does he keep himself so sweetly clean in such a land of mud! Down the outside of his brown velvet knickerbockers was the cutest little silvery-white stripe, just like that on a trooper's breeches. His tail, the train that I suppose the page carried in dancing, was remarkably long, and was decorated to match the breeches with two long white stripes, and ended in a feather duster, which was very pretty but rather overdone, I thought, until I found out that it was designed for several important purposes.

His movements were just like what one might have expected from such an elegant creature. He had touched my heart before I had seen anything but his tracks, and now he won it wholly at first meeting.

" You little beauty! You have been so invisible and mysterious that I began to hope you were a fairy, but now I see I have heard of you before. You are *Perodipus ordi*, that is sometimes called the Kangaroo Rat. I am much obliged to you for all the lace designs you have sketched and for the pretty verses you have written for me, although I could not read them all; but I am eager to have you translate them, and, in fact, am ready to sit at those microscopic and beautiful feet of yours and learn."

## II

It is of course well known that the daintiest flowers grow out of the dirt, so I was not surprised to find that the Perodipus's home is in a cave underground. No doubt those wonder-

# The Kangaroo Rat

ful eyes and long feelers were to help him in the unlighted corridors of his subterranean house.

It may seem a ruthless deed, but I was so eager to know him better that I determined to open his nest to the light of day as well as keep him a prisoner for a time, to act as my professor in Natural History.

I transferred the plush-clad atom of life to a large box that was lined with tin and half full of loose earth. Then I went out with a spade, carefully to follow and pry into the secrets of the Brownie world of which my captive was a native.

First I made a scaled diagram of the landscape concerned, for science is measurement, and exact knowledge was what I had sought since I made my choice of trails. Then I sketched the plants on the low mound. There were three large, prickly thistles, and two vigorous Spanish bayonets, or soapweeds, all of them dangerous to an unwary intruder. Next, I noticed there were nine gateways. Nine—I wonder why nine. Nine Muses? Nine lives? No, nothing of that sort (Perodipus does not live in the clouds). There were nine simply because

# The Kangaroo Rat

in this case there happened to be nine direct approaches to this Perodipus's citadel. Another might have had three, or yet another twenty-three entries, according to the needs of its owner or the locality.

Over each of the nine holes was a strong, spine-armed sentinel forever on guard and absolutely unbuyable, so that if at any time the Coyote—the Satan of the little prairie-folk—should appear among the moonlight dancers, each could dash homeward and enter by a handy door, sure that there would be standing by that door a fearless, well-armed warden, who would say to the Coyote, in a language he would well understand, "Stop! Keep off, or I'll spear you!"

And I feel very sure now that if an accident had opened a new approach, say in the direction of A, the wise little creature would also have made a handy door there for his own use. The Spanish bayonet could also keep the cattle and other heavy animals from trampling the mound, and when at night the Perodipus was making a dash for home with some fleet foe behind him, the tall, dark form of the friendly bayonet would be his landmark in the uncertain

243.

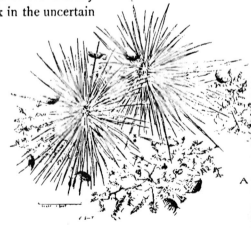

A

# The Kangaroo Rat

light. In summer-time, I now remembered, when other plants were not dead, as at present, the bayonet, in its sombre evergreen, would be a poor landmark by night; but it meets the new necessity in a splendid way. Out of its bristling topmost serried spears it sends far up into the purple night a wondrous candelabrum on a towering pole, with flowers of shining white, that must loom up afar, like some new constellation in the sky. And so the Perodipus's safety-port is lighthoused day and night.

I began carefully to open up the main gallery to the home of my moonlight dancer, and had not gone very far when I came on something that made me jump; nothing less than a ferocious-looking reptile—the *Huajalote*, that the Mexicans hold in superstitious and mortal dread, the *Amblystoma* of scientists. It was only a small one, but it gave me the creeps to see him lashing his venomous-looking tail and oozing all over with a poisonous slime. If he could affect me so much, what might he be like to the gentle little Perodipus, whose home he seemed trying to raid? But for some reason that I did not understand then, the reptile was boring his

A Ferocious-looking Reptile.

# The Kangaroo Rat

nose into a solid bank of sand that was the end
of the gallery he had entered by. Since we
were all playing " fairy-tale," I, the Giant, did
not hesitate to put the Dragon where he could
harm the fairies no longer.

After hours of patient digging and measuring
I got a map of the underground world where
the Perodipus passes the daytime.

The central chamber could be *nearly* reached
by any of the entrances, but one not knowing
the secret would have passed by and come
out into the air again at another door. No
matter how often he went in, he never would
have found the nest or any of the real treasure
of the home, for the road to the nest was plugged
with earth each time the owner left it.

And this is exactly what happened to the
Huajalote; for he seemed to have an idea that
there was a secret passage if he only could find it,
and no doubt thought it was somewhere through
the bank of earth he was boring into, though
really he was not anywhere near to the spot.

I think the chamber was not shut off from
the air, for the small round hole X (see page
243) was, I suspect, its air-shaft, though I am

247

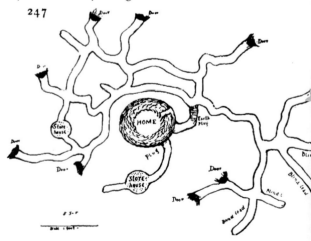

not sure of this, for the roof caved in before I could examine it fully.

The chamber itself was very large, being twelve inches long and eight inches wide, with a high vaulted roof at least over five inches from the floor, and ribbed with the living roots of the grand old bayonet-trees at the door. Having discovered the entry to it, I thought I was in the nest; but not so. I was stopped now by a mass of interlaced, spiny grasses that would probably have turned the Huajalote had he gotten so far. After I had forced my way through this I found that the real entrance was cleverly hidden near a corner. Then there was a thick felting of fine grass and weed silk, and inside of all a lining of softest feathers. I think that every gay little Bird on the plains must have contributed one of its finest feathers to that nest, for it was as soft and pretty and warm as it should have been for the cradle of those pinky-white seed-pearls that the Perodipus's babies are when first they come from the land of the Stars and the Stork into their underground home.

Down in one corner of this Great Hall I

## The Kangaroo Rat

found signs of another secret passage. It was
like exploring a mediæval castle. This passage
went down at a slant when I got fairly into it,
and before long it opened out into a large storehouse that was filled with over a pint of seeds
of the prairie sunflower. This room was sunken
deepest of all in the ground, and was also in
the shadiest part of the mound, so that the seed
would be in no danger of heating or sprouting.
At one end of this chamber was another blind
lead that possibly was used in filling the ware-
house and afterward sealed up for safety. There
were many of these blind alleys. They appeared to be either entrances plugged up or else
deliberate plans to mislead an intruder who did
not have the key to the secret door.

Yet one more chamber was found, and that
was a second storehouse, a reserve supply of
carefully selected helianthus seeds, about half a
gill of them, and yet not a bad one or a shriv-
elled one was to be found in the lot.

But I did not find any of the Perodipus family,
and think it possible that when they heard my
rude approach they all escaped by some other
secret passage that I failed to discover.

# The Kangaroo Rat

This was the home of my nightly visitor, planned and carried out with wisdom for all the straits of his daily life and near future.

## III

ITS owner in the cage I now watched with double interest. He was the embodiment of restless energy, palpitating with life from the tip of his translucent nose and ears to the end of his vibrant tail. He could cross the box at a single bound, and I now saw the purpose of his huge tail. In the extraordinary long flying leaps that Perodipus makes, the tuft on the end does for him what the feathers do for an arrow. It keeps him straight in the air on his trajectory. But it does more, for it enables him slightly to change his course if he finds it wiser after he has leaped. And the tail itself has other uses. The Perodipus has no pocket in his striped trousers to carry home his winter supplies, but he has capacious pockets, one in each cheek, which he can fill till they bulge out wider than himself—so wide that he must turn his head sidewise to enter his own front gate.

# The Kangaroo Rat

Such a load added to his head totally displaces his centre of gravity, which is adjusted for leaping with empty pockets. But here is where the tail comes in. Its great length and size make it a powerful lever, and by raising it to different angles he accommodates himself to his load and leaps along in perfect poise in spite of a week's provision in his cheeks.

He was the most indefatigable little miner that I ever saw. Those pinky-white paws, not much larger than a pencil-point, seemed never weary of digging, and would send the earth out between his hind legs in little jets like a steam-shovel. He seemed tireless at his work. He first tunnelled the whole mass through and through, and, I doubt not, made and unmade several ideal underground residences, and solved many problems of rapid underground transit. Then he embarked in some landscape-gardening schemes and made it his nightly business to change entirely the geography of his whole country, laboriously making hills and cañons wheresoever seemed unto him good.

There was one landscape effect that he seemed very fond of. That was a sort of Colorado

# The Kangaroo Rat

Cañon with the San Francisco Mountain on its edge. He tried a long time to use a certain large stone for a peak to his mountain, but it was past his strength, and he resented, rather than profited by, any help I gave him. This stone gave him endless trouble for a time. He could not use it, nor even get rid of it, until he discovered that he could at least dig the earth from under it, and so keep it going down, until finally it settled at the bottom of the box and troubled him no more.

He used to take a lot of comfort out of jumping clear from the top of the Frisco Peak across the Grand Cañon into Utah (two hundred miles), at the other side of the box, and back home again to the Peak (six thousand feet).

I watched, sketched, and studied him as well as I could, considering his shyness and nocturnal habits, and I learned daily to admire him more. His untiring devotion to his nightly geographical lesson was marvellous. His talent for heaving up new mountain-ranges was astonishing, positively volcanic. When first I suspected his existence, I had been willing to call

# The Kangaroo Rat

him a fairy. When I saw him I said, " Why, it's only a Kangaroo Rat." But after I had watched him a couple of weeks in the cage I realized fully that millions of little creatures with such energy, working for thousands of years, could not but change the whole surface of a country, by letting in the frost and rain, as well as by their own work. Then I was obliged to concede that Perodipus was more than Rat or Brownie; he was nothing less than a Geological Epoch.

## IV

THERE was one more lesson, a great surprise, in store for me. It is well known to scientists that the common House-mouse has a song not unlike that of some Birds. Occasionally gifted individuals are found that fill our closet or cellar with midnight music that a Canary might be proud of. Further investigations have shown that the common Deer-mouse of the Eastern woods also is a gifted vocalist.

Now, any cow-boy on the upland plains will tell you that at night, when sleeping out, he has

## The Kangaroo Rat

often heard the most curious strains of birdy music in his half-awakening hours,—a soft, sweet twittering song with trills and deeper notes,—and if he thought about it at all he set it down to some small Bird singing in its dreams, or accepted his comrade's unexplanatory explanation that it was one of those "prairie nightingales." But what that was he did not trouble himself to know.

I have often heard the strange night song, but not being able to trace it home, I set it down to some little Bird that was too happy to express it all in daylight hours.

Several times at night I overheard from my captive a long-drawn note, before it dawned on me that this was the same voice as that which often sings to the rising moon. I did not hear him really sing, I am sorry to say. I have no final proof. My captive was not seeking to amuse me. Indeed, his attitude toward me from first to last was one of unbending scorn. I can only say I *think* (and hope) that it was the same voice. But my allegiance is due to exact science. Oh, why did I not take the other trail? For then I should have been able to announce

254

# The Kangaroo Rat

here, as now I do not dare to, that the sweet night singer of the plains and the plush-clad fairy that nightly danced about my door *are the same*.

But one night there was a fresh upheaval of Nature, and my Immeasurable Force tried a new experiment in terrestrial convulsions. He started his mountain, not in the middle of his kingdom, as aforetime, but afar to the southwest, in one corner of the box, and a notable mountain he made. He simply ruined the Grand Cañon to use the material of its walls.

Higher and higher those tiny pink pawlets piled the beetling crags, and the dizzy peak arose above the sinking plain as it never had before.

It went up fast, too, for it was in the angle of the box, and it was rapidly nearing the heaven of heavens represented by the lid, when an accident turned the current of the Perodipus's ambitions. He was now at an altitude that he had never before reached since his imprisonment, so high that he could touch the narrow strip of the wooden walls that was unprotected by the tin. The new substance tempted his teeth. Oh, new-found joy! it was

R

easy to cut. He set to work with his usual energy, and in a very short time cut his way through the half-inch pine, then escaped from the tin-clad kingdom that had been forced upon him, and its Geological Epoch was gone. My professor had quit his chair. I had been willing to find an impossible mystery, but I had found a delightful story from Nature's wonderland.

## V

AND now he is once more skimming merrily over the mud and sands of the upland plains; shooting across the open like a living, feathered arrow; tempting the rash Coyote to thrust his unfortunate nose into those awful cactus brakes, or teaching the Prairie Owls that if they do not let him alone they will surely come to grief on a Spanish bayonet; coming out by night again to scribble his lacework designs on the smooth places, to write verses of measured rhythm, or to sing and play hop-scotch in the moonlight with his merry crew.

Soft as a shadow, swift as an arrow, dainty as thistle-down, bright-eyed and beautiful, with a

Shooting Across the Open Like an Arrow.

# The Kangaroo Rat

secret way to an underground world where he
finds safety from his foes—my first impression
was not so very far astray. I had surely found
the Little Folk, and nearer, better, and more
human Little Folk than any in the nursery
books. My chosen flinty track had led me on
to Upper Arcadie at last. And now, when I
hear certain purblind folk talk of Fairies and
Brownies as a race peculiar to the romantic
parts of England, Ireland, or India, I think:

" *You* have been wasting your time reading
books. You have never been on the shifting
Currumpaw when the moon of the Mesas comes
up to glint the river at its every bend, and bathe
the hills in green and veil the shades in blue.
You have not heard the moonlight music. You
have not seen these moonbeams skip from
thistle-top and bayonet-spear to rest in peace at
last, as by appointment, on the smooth-swept
dancing-floor of a tiny race that visits this earth
each night, coming from nowhere, and disap-
pearing without a sound of falling feet.

" You have never seen this, for you have not
found the key to the secret chamber; and if
you did, you still might doubt, for the dainty

## The Kangaroo Rat

moonlight revellers have coats of darkness and become invisible at will.

"Indeed, I believe you would say the whole thing was a dream. But what about the lace traceries in the dust? They are there when the sun comes up next morning."

Tempting the Rash Coyote.

Tito:

The Story of the Coyote that Learned How

# Tito:

## The Story of the Coyote that Learned How

### I

A RAINDROP may deflect a thunderbolt, or a hair may ruin an empire, as surely as a spider-web once turned the history of Scotland; and if it had not been for one little pebble, this history of Tito might never have happened.

That pebble was lying on a trail in the Dakota Badlands, and one hot, dark night it lodged in the foot of a Horse that was ridden by a tipsy cow-boy. The man got off, as a matter of habit, to know what was laming his Horse. But he left the reins on its neck instead of on the ground, and the Horse, taking advantage of this technicality, ran off in the darkness. Then the cow-boy, realizing that he was afoot, lay down in a hollow under some buffalo-bushes and slept the loggish sleep of the befuddled.

THE golden beams of the early summer sun were leaping from top to top of the wonderful Badland Buttes, when an old Coyote might have been seen trotting homeward along the Garner's Creek Trail with a Rabbit in her jaws to supply her family's breakfast.

Fierce war had for a long time been waged against the Coyote kind by the cattlemen of Billings County. Traps, guns, poison, and Hounds had reduced their number nearly to zero, and the few survivors had learned the bitter need of caution at every step. But the destructive ingenuity of man knew no bounds, and their numbers continued to dwindle.

The old Coyote quit the trail very soon, for nothing that man has made is friendly. She skirted along a low ridge, then across a little hollow where grew a few buffalo-bushes, and, after a careful sniff at a very stale human trail-scent, she crossed another near ridge on whose

266

sunny side was the home of her brood. Again she cautiously circled, peered about, and sniffed, but, finding no sign of danger, went down to the doorway and uttered a low *woof-woof*. Out of the den, beside a sage-bush, there poured a procession of little Coyotes, merrily tumbling over one another. Then, barking little barks and growling little puppy growls, they fell upon the feast that their mother had brought, and gobbled and tussled while she looked on and enjoyed their joy.

Wolver Jake, the cow-boy, had awakened from his chilly sleep about sunrise, in time to catch a glimpse of the Coyote passing over the ridge. As soon as she was out of sight he got on his feet and went to the edge, there to witness the interesting scene of the family breakfasting and frisking about within a few yards of him, utterly unconscious of any danger.

But the only appeal the scene had to him lay in the fact that the county had set a price on every one of these Coyotes' lives. So he got out his big 45 navy revolver, and notwithstanding his shaky condition, he managed somehow to get a sight on the mother as she

was caressing one of the little ones that had finished its breakfast, and shot her dead on the spot.

The terrified cubs fled into the den, and Jake, failing to kill another with his revolver, came forward, blocked up the hole with stones, and leaving the seven little prisoners quaking at the far end, set off on foot for the nearest ranch, cursing his faithless Horse as he went.

In the afternoon he returned with his pard and tools for digging. The little ones had cowered all day in the darkened hole, wondering why their mother did not come to feed them, wondering at the darkness and the change. But late that day they heard sounds at the door. Then light was again let in. Some of the less cautious young ones ran forward to meet their mother, but their mother was not there—only two great rough brutes that began tearing open their home.

After an hour or more the diggers came to the end of the den, and here were the woolly, bright-eyed, little ones, all huddled in a pile at the farthest corner. Their innocent puppy faces and ways were not noticed by the huge

enemy. One by one they were seized. A
sharp blow, and each quivering, limp form
was thrown into a sack to be carried to the
nearest magistrate who was empowered to pay
the bounties.

Even at this age there was a certain individuality of character among the puppies. Some
of them squealed and some of them growled
when dragged out to die. One or two tried to
bite. The one that had been slowest to comprehend the danger, had been the last to retreat,
and so was on top of the pile, and therefore the
first killed. The one that had first realized the
peril had retreated first, and now crouched at
the bottom of the pile. Coolly and remorselessly the others were killed one by one, and
then this prudent little puppy was seen to be
the last of the family. It lay perfectly still,
even when touched, its eyes being half closed,
as, guided by instinct, it tried to "play possum."
One of the men picked it up. It neither
squealed nor resisted. Then Jake, realizing
ever the importance of "standing in with the
boss," said: "Say, let's keep that 'un for the
children." So the last of the family was thrown

269

alive into the same bag with its dead brothers, and, bruised and frightened, lay there very still, understanding nothing, knowing only that after a long time of great noise and cruel jolting it was again half strangled by a grip on its neck and dragged out, where were a lot of creatures like the diggers.

These were really the inhabitants of the Chimney-pot Ranch, whose brand is the Broad-arrow; and among them were the children for whom the cub had been brought. The boss had no difficulty in getting Jake to accept the dollar that the cub Coyote would have brought in bounty-money, and his present was turned over to the children. In answer to their question, " What is it? " a Mexican cow-hand present said it was a Coyotito,—that is, a " little Coyote,"—and this, afterward shortened to " Tito," became the captive's name.

## II

TITO was a pretty little creature, with woolly body, a puppy-like expression, and a head that was singularly broad between the ears.

Coyotito, the Captive.

But, as a children's pet, she—for it proved
to be a female—was not a success. She was
distant and distrustful. She ate her food and
seemed healthy, but never responded to friendly
advances; never even learned to come out of
the box when called. This probably was due
to the fact that the kindness of the small children was offset by the roughness of the men
and boys, who did not hesitate to drag her out
by the chain when they wished to see her. On
these occasions she would suffer in silence,
playing possum, shamming dead, for she seemed
to know that that was the best thing to do. But
as soon as released she would once more retire
into the darkest corner of her box, and watch
her tormentors with eyes that, at the proper
angle, showed a telling glint of green.

Among the children of the ranchmen was a
thirteen-year-old boy. The fact that he grew
up to be like his father, a kind, strong, and
thoughtful man, did not prevent him being, at
this age, a shameless little brute.

Like all boys in that country, he practised
lasso-throwing, with a view to being a cow-boy.
Posts and stumps are uninteresting things to

catch.  His little brothers and sisters were under special protection of the Home Government. The Dogs ran far away whenever they saw him coming with the rope in his hands.  So he must needs practise on the unfortunate Coyotito.  She soon learned that her only hope for peace was to hide in the kennel, or, if thrown at when outside, to dodge the rope by lying as flat as possible on the ground.  Thus Lincoln unwittingly taught the Coyote the dangers and limitations of a rope, and so he proved a blessing in disguise—a very perfect disguise.  When the Coyote had thoroughly learned how to baffle the lasso, the boy terror devised a new amusement.  He got a large trap of the kind known as " Fox-size."  This he set in the dust as he had seen Jake set a Wolf-trap, close to the kennel, and over it he scattered scraps of meat, in the most approved style for Wolf-trapping. After a while Tito, drawn by the smell of the meat, came hungrily sneaking out toward it, and almost immediately was caught in the trap by one foot.  The boy terror was watching from a near hiding-place.  He gave a wild Indian whoop of delight, then rushed forward

to drag the Coyote out of the box into which she had retreated. After some more delightful thrills of excitement and struggle he got his lasso on Tito's body, and, helped by a younger brother, a most promising pupil, he succeeded in setting the Coyote free from the trap before the grown-ups had discovered his amusement. One or two experiences like this taught her a mortal terror of traps. She soon learned the smell of the steel, and could detect and avoid it, no matter how cleverly Master Lincoln might bury it in the dust, while the younger brother screened the operation from the intended victim by holding his coat over the door of Tito's kennel.

One day the fastening of her chain gave way, and Tito went off in an uncertain fashion, trailing her chain behind her. But she was seen by one of the men, who fired a charge of bird-shot at her. The burning, stinging, and surprise of it all caused her to retreat to the one place she knew, her own kennel. The chain was fastened again, and Tito added to her ideas this, a horror of guns and the smell of gunpowder; and this also, that the one safety from them is to "lay low."

## Tito

There were yet other rude experiences in store for the captive.

Poisoning Wolves was a topic of daily talk at the Ranch, so it was not surprising that Lincoln should privately experiment on Coyotito. The deadly strychnine was too well guarded to be available. So Lincoln hid some Rough on Rats in a piece of meat, threw it to the captive, and sat by to watch, as blithe and conscience-clear as any professor of chemistry trying a new combination.

Tito smelled the meat—everything had to be passed on by her nose. Her nose was in doubt. There was a good smell of meat, a familiar but unpleasant smell of human hands, and a strange new odor, but not the odor of the trap; so she bolted the morsel. Within a few minutes she began to have fearful pains in her stomach, followed by cramps. Now in all the Wolf tribe there is the instinctive habit to throw up anything that disagrees with them, and after a minute or two of suffering the Coyote sought relief in this way; and to make it doubly sure she hastily gobbled some blades of grass, and in less than an hour was quite well again.

276

# Tito

Lincoln had put in poison enough for a dozen Coyotes. Had he put in less she could not have felt the pang till too late, but she recovered and never forgot that peculiar smell that means such awful after-pains. More than that, she was ready thenceforth to fly at once to the herbal cure that Nature had everywhere provided. An instinct of this kind grows quickly, once followed. It had taken minutes of suffering in the first place to drive her to the easement. Thenceforth, having learned, it was her first thought on feeling pain. The little miscreant did indeed succeed in having her swallow another bait with a small dose of poison, but she knew what to do now and had almost no suffering.

Later on, a relative sent Lincoln a Bull-terrier, and the new combination was a fresh source of spectacular interest for the boy, and of tribulation for the Coyote. It all emphasized for her that old idea to "lay low"—that is, to be quiet, unobtrusive, and hide when danger is in sight. The grown-ups of the household at length forbade these persecutions, and the Terrier was kept away from the little yard where the Coyote was chained up.

277

It must not be supposed that, in all this, Tito was a sweet, innocent victim. She had learned to bite. She had caught and killed several chickens by shamming sleep while they ventured to forage within the radius of her chain. And she had an inborn hankering to sing a morning and evening hymn, which procured for her many beatings. But she learned to shut up, the moment her opening notes were followed by a rattle of doors or windows, for these sounds of human nearness had frequently been followed by a *"bang"* and a charge of bird-shot, which somehow did no serious harm, though it severely stung her hide. And these experiences all helped to deepen her terror of guns and of those who used them. The object of these musical outpourings was not clear. They happened usually at dawn or dusk, but sometimes a loud noise at high noon would set her going. The song consisted of a volley of short barks, mixed with doleful squalls that never failed to set the Dogs astir in a responsive uproar, and once or twice had begotten a far-away answer from some wild Coyote in the hills.

There was one little trick that she had de-

veloped which was purely instinctive—that is,
an inherited habit. In the back end of her
kennel she had a little *cache* of bones, and knew
exactly where one or two lumps of unsavory
meat were buried within the radius of her chain,
for a time of famine which never came. If any
one approached these hidden treasures she
watched with anxious eyes, but made no other
demonstration. If she saw that the meddler
knew the exact place, she took an early opportunity to secrete them elsewhere.

After a year of this life Tito had grown to
full size, and had learned many things that her
wild kinsmen could not have learned without
losing their lives in doing it. She knew and
feared traps. She had learned to avoid poison
baits, and knew what to do at once if, by some
mistake, she should take one. She knew what
guns are. She had learned to cut her morning
and evening song very short. She had some
acquaintance with Dogs, enough to make her
hate and distrust them all. But, above all, she
had this idea: whenever danger is near, the
very best move possible is to lay low, be very
quiet, do nothing to attract notice. Perhaps

the little brain that looked out of those changing yellow eyes was the storehouse of much
other knowledge about men, but what it was
did not appear.

The Coyote was fully grown when the boss
of the outfit bought a couple of thoroughbred
Greyhounds, wonderful runners, to see whether
he could not entirely extirpate the remnant of
the Coyotes that still destroyed occasional
Sheep and Calves on the range, and at the same
time find amusement in the sport.   He was tired
of seeing that Coyote in the yard ; so, deciding
to use her for training the Dogs, he had her
roughly thrown into a bag, then carried a quarter of a mile away and dumped out.   At the
same time the Greyhounds were slipped and
chivvied on.   Away they went bounding at
their matchless pace, that nothing else on four
legs could equal, and away went the Coyote,
frightened by the noise of the men, frightened
even to find herself free.   Her quarter-mile
start quickly shrank to one hundred yards, the
one hundred to fifty, and on sped the flying
Dogs.   Clearly there was no chance for her.
On and nearer they came.   In another minute

she would have been stretched out—not a
doubt of it. But on a sudden she stopped,
turned, and walked toward the Dogs with her
tail serenely waving in the air and a friendly
cock to her ears. Greyhounds are peculiar
Dogs. Anything that runs away, they are going
to catch and kill if they can. Anything that is
calmly facing them becomes at once a non-
combatant. They bounded over and past the
Coyote before they could curb their own im-
petuosity, and returned completely nonplussed.
Possibly they recognized the Coyote of the
house-yard as she stood there wagging her tail.
The ranchmen were nonplussed too. Every
one was utterly taken aback, had a sense of
failure, and the real victor in the situation was
felt to be the audacious little Coyote.

The Greyhounds refused to attack an animal
that wagged its tail and would not run; and
the men, on seeing that the Coyote could *walk*
far enough away to avoid being caught by hand,
took their ropes (lassoes), and soon made her a
prisoner once more.

The next day they decided to try again, but
this time they added the white Bull-terrier to

281

the chasers. The Coyote did as before. The Greyhounds declined to be party to any attack on such a mild and friendly acquaintance. But the Bull-terrier, who came puffing and panting on the scene three minutes later, had no such scruples. He was not so tall, but he was heavier than the Coyote, and, seizing her by her wool-protected neck, he shook her till, in a surprisingly short time, she lay limp and lifeless, at which all the men seemed pleased, and congratulated the Terrier, while the Greyhounds pottered around in restless perplexity.

A stranger in the party, a newly arrived Englishman, asked if he might have the brush,—the tail, he explained,—and on being told to help himself, he picked up the victim by the tail, and with one awkward chop of his knife he cut it off at the middle, and the Coyote dropped, but gave a shrill yelp of pain. She was not dead, only playing possum, and now she leaped up and vanished into a near-by thicket of cactus and sage.

With Greyhounds a running animal is the signal for a run, so the two long-legged Dogs and the white, broad-chested Dog dashed after

282

the Coyote. But right across their path, by
happy chance, there flashed a brown streak
ridden by a snowy powder-puff, the visible but
evanescent sign for Cottontail Rabbit. The
Coyote was not in sight now. The Rabbit
was, so the Greyhounds dashed after the Cottontail, who took advantage of a Prairie-dog's
hole to seek safety in the bosom of Mother
Earth, and the Coyote made good her escape.

She had been a good deal jarred by the rude
treatment of the Terrier, and her mutilated tail
gave her some pain. But otherwise she was
all right, and she loped lightly away, keeping
out of sight in the hollows, and so escaped
among the fantastic buttes of the Badlands, to
be eventually the founder of a new life among
the Coyotes of the Little Missouri.

Moses was preserved by the Egyptians till he
had outlived the dangerous period, and learned
from them wisdom enough to be the savior of
his people against those same Egyptians. So
the bobtailed Coyote was not only saved by
man and carried over the dangerous period of
puppyhood: she was also unwittingly taught by
him how to baffle the traps, poisons, lassos,

guns, and Dogs that had so long waged a war
of extermination against her race.

### III

THUS Tito escaped from man, and for the first
time found herself face to face with the whole
problem of life; for now she had her own living
to get.

A wild animal has three sources of wisdom:

First, *the experience of its ancestors*, in the
form of instinct, which is inborn learning, ham-
mered into the race by ages of selection and
tribulation. This is the most important to
begin with, because it guards him from the
moment he is born.

Second, *the experience of his parents and comrades*, learned chiefly by example. This becomes most important as soon as the young
can run.

Third, *the personal experience* of the animal
itself. This grows in importance as the animal
ages.

The weakness of the first is its fixity; it
cannot change to meet quickly changing condi-

tions. The weakness of the second is the animal's inability freely to exchange ideas by language. The weakness of the third is the danger in acquiring it. But the three together are a strong arch.

Now, Tito was in a new case. Perhaps never before had a Coyote faced life with unusual advantages in the third kind of knowledge, none at all in the second, and with the first dormant. She travelled rapidly away from the ranchmen, keeping out of sight, and sitting down once in a while to lick her wounded tail-stump. She came at last to a Prairie-dog town. Many of the inhabitants were out, and they barked at the intruder, but all dodged down as soon as she came near. Her instinct taught her to try and catch one, but she ran about in vain for some time, and then gave it up. She would have gone hungry that night but that she found a couple of Mice in the long grass by the river. Her mother had not taught her to hunt, but her instinct did, and the accident that she had an unusual brain made her profit very quickly by her experience.

In the days that followed she quickly learned

how to make a living; for Mice, Ground Squirrels, Prairie-dogs, Rabbits, and Lizards were
abundant, and many of these could be captured
in open chase. But open chase, and sneaking
as near as possible before beginning the open
chase, lead naturally to stalking for a final spring.
And before the moon had changed the Coyote
had learned how to make a comfortable living.

Once or twice she saw the men with the Greyhounds coming her way. Most Coyotes would,
perhaps, have barked in bravado, or would have
gone up to some high place whence they could
watch the enemy; but Tito did no such foolish
thing. Had she run, her moving form would
have caught the eyes of the Dogs, and then
nothing could have saved her. She dropped
where she was, and lay flat until the danger
had passed. Thus her ranch training to lay
low began to stand her in good stead, and
so it came about that her weakness was her
strength. The Coyote kind had so long been
famous for their speed, had so long learned to
trust in their legs, that they never dreamed of a
creature that could run them down. They were
accustomed to play with their pursuers, and so

rarely bestirred themselves to run from Greyhounds, till it was too late. But Tito, brought up at the end of a chain, was a poor runner. She had no reason to trust her legs. She rather trusted her wits, and so lived.

During that summer she stayed about the Little Missouri, learning the tricks of small-game hunting that she should have learned before she shed her milk-teeth, and gaining in strength and speed. She kept far away from all the ranches, and always hid on seeing a man or a strange beast, and so passed the summer alone. During the daytime she was not lonely, but when the sun went down she would feel the impulse to sing that wild song of the West which means so much to the Coyotes.

It is not the invention of an individual nor of the present, but was slowly built out of the feelings of all Coyotes in all ages. It expresses their nature and the Plains that made their nature. When one begins it, it takes hold of the rest, as the fife and drum do with soldiers, or the ki-yi war-song with Indian braves. They respond to it as a bell-glass does to a certain note the moment that note is struck, ignoring

287

T

other sounds. So the Coyote, no matter how brought up, must vibrate at the night song of the Plains, for it touches something in himself.

They sing it after sundown, when it becomes the rallying-cry of their race and the friendly call to a neighbor; and they sing it as one boy in the woods holloas to another to say, " All's well! Here am I. Where are you? " A form of it they sing to the rising moon, for this is the time for good hunting to begin. They sing when they see the new camp-fire, for the same reason that a Dog barks at a stranger. Yet another weird chant they have for the dawning before they steal quietly away from the offing of the camp—a wild, weird, squalling refrain:

Wow-wow-wow-wow-wow-w-o-o-o-o-o-w,

again and again; and doubtless with many another change that man cannot distinguish any more than the Coyote can distinguish the words in the cow-boy's anathemas.

Tito instinctively uttered her music at the proper times. But sad experiences had taught her to cut it short and keep it low. Once or twice she had got a far-away reply from one of her own race, whereupon she had quickly ceased and timidly quit the neighborhood.

One day, when on the Upper Garner's Creek, she found the trail where a piece of meat had been dragged along. It was a singularly inviting odor, and she followed it, partly out of curiosity. Presently she came on a piece of the meat itself. She was hungry; she was always hungry now. It was tempting, and although it had a peculiar odor, she swallowed it. Within a few minutes she felt a terrific pain. The memory of the poisoned meat the boy had given her, was fresh. With trembling, foaming jaws she seized some blades of grass, and her stomach threw off the meat; but she fell in convulsions on the ground.

The trail of meat dragged along and the poison baits had been laid the day before by Wolver Jake. This morning he was riding the drag, and on coming up from the draw he saw, far ahead, the Coyote struggling. He knew, of course, that it was poisoned, and rode quickly up; but the convulsions passed as he neared. By a mighty effort, at the sound of the Horses' hoofs the Coyote arose to her front feet. Jake drew his revolver and fired, but the only effect was fully to alarm her. She tried to run, but her hind legs were paralyzed. She put forth all her strength, dragging her hind legs. Now, when the poison was no longer in the stomach, will-power could do a great deal. Had she been allowed to lie down then she would have been dead in five minutes; but the revolver-shots and the man coming stirred her to strenuous action. Madly she struggled again and again to get her hind legs to work. All the force of desperate intent she brought to bear. It was like putting forth tenfold power to force the nervous fluids through their blocked-up channels as she dragged herself with marvellous speed downhill. What is nerve but will? The dead wires of her legs were hot with this fresh power, multiplied, injected, blasted into them. They had to give in. She felt them thrill with life again. Each wild shot from the gun lent vital help. Another fierce attempt, and one hind leg obeyed the call to duty. A few more bounds, and the other, too, fell in. Then lightly she loped away among the broken buttes,

defying the agonizing gripe that still kept on inside.

Had Jake held off then she would yet have laid down and died; but he followed, and fired and fired, till in another mile she bounded free from pain, saved from her enemy by himself. He had compelled her to take the only cure, so she escaped.

And these were the ideas that she harvested that day: That curious smell on the meat stands for mortal agony. Let it alone! And she never forgot it; thenceforth she knew strychnine.

Fortunately, Dogs, traps, and strychnine do not wage war at once, for the Dogs are as apt to be caught or poisoned as the Coyotes. Had there been a single Dog in the hunt that day Tito's history would have ended.

## IV

WHEN the weather grew cooler toward the end of autumn Tito had gone far toward repairing the defects in her early training. She was more like an ordinary Coyote in her habits now, and she was more disposed to sing the sundown song.

One night, when she got a response, she yielded to the impulse again to call, and soon afterward a large, dark Coyote appeared. The fact that he was there at all was a guarantee of unusual gifts, for the war against his race was waged relentlessly by the cattlemen. He approached with caution. Tito's mane bristled with mixed feelings at the sight of one of her own kind. She crouched flat on the ground and waited. The newcomer came stiffly forward, nosing the wind; then up the wind nearly to her. Then he walked around so that she should wind him, and raising his tail, gently waved it. The first acts meant armed neutrality, but the last was a distinctly friendly signal. Then he approached, and she rose up suddenly and stood as high as she could to be smelled. Then she wagged the stump of her tail, and they considered themselves acquainted.

The newcomer was a very large Coyote, half as tall again as Tito, and the dark patch on his shoulders was so large and black that the cow-boys, when they came to know him, called him Saddleback. From that time these two continued more or less together. They were

They Considered Themselves Acquainted.

# Tito

not always close together, often were miles apart during the day, but toward night one or the other would get on some high, open place and sing the loud

Yap-yap-yap-yow-wow-wow-wow-wow,

and they would forgather for some foray on hand.

The physical advantages were with Saddleback, but the greater cunning was Tito's, so that she in time became the leader. Before a month a third Coyote had appeared on the scene and become also a member of this loose-bound fraternity, and later two more appeared. Nothing succeeds like success. The little bob-tailed Coyote had had rare advantages of training just where the others were lacking: she knew the devices of man. She could not tell about these in words, but she could by the aid of a few signs and a great deal of example. It soon became evident that her methods of hunting were successful, whereas, when they went without her, they often had hard luck. A man at Boxelder Ranch had twenty Sheep. The rules of the county did not allow any one to

295

own more, as this was a Cattle-range. The Sheep were guarded by a large and fierce Collie. One day in winter two of the Coyotes tried to raid this flock by a bold dash, and all they got was a mauling from the Collie. A few days later the band returned at dusk. Just how Tito arranged it, man cannot tell. We can only guess how she taught them their parts, but we know that she surely did. The Coyotes hid in the willows. Then Saddleback, the bold and swift, walked openly toward the Sheep and barked a loud defiance. The Collie jumped up with bristling mane and furious growl, then, seeing the foe, dashed straight at him. Now was the time for the steady nerve and the unfailing limbs. Saddleback let the Dog come near enough *almost* to catch him, and so beguiled him far and away into the woods, while the other Coyotes, led by Tito, stampeded the Sheep in twenty directions; then following the farthest, they killed several and left them in the snow.

In the gloom of descending night the Dog and his master labored till they had gathered the bleating survivors; but next morning they

296

found that four had been driven far away and killed, and the Coyotes had had a banquet royal.

The shepherd poisoned the carcasses and left them. Next night the Coyotes returned. Tito sniffed the now frozen meat, detected the poison, gave a warning growl, and scattered filth over the meat, so that none of the band should touch it. One, however, who was fast and foolish, persisted in feeding in spite of Tito's warning, and when they came away he was lying poisoned and dead in the snow.

## V

JAKE now heard on all sides that the Coyotes were getting worse. So he set to work with many traps and much poison to destroy those on the Garner's Creek, and every little while he would go with the Hounds and scour the Little Missouri south and east of the Chimney-pot Ranch; for it was understood that he must never run the Dogs in country where traps and poison were laid. He worked in his erratic way all winter, and certainly did have some success. He killed a couple of gray Wolves, said to be the last of their race, and several Coyotes, some of which, no doubt, were of the Bobtailed pack, which thereby lost those members which were lacking in wisdom.

Yet that winter was marked by a series of Coyote raids and exploits; and usually the track in the snow or the testimony of eye-witnesses told that the master spirit of it all was a little Bobtailed Coyote.

One of these adventures was the cause of much talk. The Coyote challenge sounded close to the Chimney-pot Ranch after sun-down. A dozen Dogs responded with the usual clamor. But only the Bull-terrier dashed away toward the place whence the Coyotes had called, for the reason that he only was loose. His chase was fruitless, and he came back growling. Twenty minutes later there was another Coyote yell close at hand. Off dashed the Terrier as before. In a minute his excited yapping told that he had sighted his game and was in full chase. Away he went, furiously barking, until his voice was lost afar, and nevermore was heard. In the morning the men read in

the snow the tale of the night. The first cry
of the Coyotes was to find out if all the Dogs
were loose; then, having found that only one
was free, they laid a plan. Five Coyotes hid
along the side of the trail; one went forward
and called till it had decoyed the rash Terrier,
and then led him right into the ambush. What
chance had he with six? They tore him limb
from limb, and devoured him, too, at the very
spot where once he had worried Coyotito. And
next morning, when the men came, they saw by
the signs that the whole thing had been planned,
and that the leader whose cunning had made it
a success was a little Bobtailed Coyote.

The men were angry, and Lincoln was furi-
ous; but Jake remarked: "Well, I guess that
Bobtail came back and got even with that
Terrier."

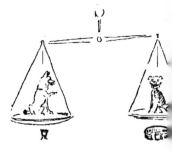

## VI

WHEN spring was near, the annual love-season
of the Coyotes came on. Saddleback and Tito
had been together merely as companions all
winter, but now a new feeling was born. There
was not much courting. Saddleback simply

showed his teeth to possible rivals. There was no ceremony. They had been friends for months, and now, in the light of the new feeling, they naturally took to each other and were mated. Coyotes do not give each other names as do mankind, but have one sound like a growl and short howl, which stands for "mate" or "husband" or "wife." This they use in calling to each other, and it is by recognizing the tone of the voice that they know who is calling.

The loose rambling brotherhood of the Coyotes was broken up now, for the others also paired off, and since the returning warm weather was bringing out the Prairie-dogs and small game, there was less need to combine for hunting. Ordinarily Coyotes do not sleep in dens or in any fixed place. They move about all night while it is cool, then during the daytime they get a few hours' sleep in the sun, on some quiet hillside that also gives a chance to watch out. But the mating season changes this habit somewhat.

As the weather grew warm Tito and Saddleback set about preparing a den for the expected

Their Evening Song.

family.   In a warm little hollow, an old Badger
abode was cleaned out, enlarged, and deepened.
A quantity of leaves and grass was carried into
it and arranged in a comfortable nest.   The
place selected for it was a dry, sunny nook
among the hills, half a mile west of the Little
Missouri.   Thirty yards from it was a ridge
which commanded a wide view of the grassy
slopes and cottonwood groves by the river.
Men would have called the spot very beautiful,
but it is tolerably certain that that side of it
never touched the Coyotes at all.

Tito began to be much preoccupied with her
impending duties.   She stayed quietly in the
neighborhood of the den, and lived on such food
as Saddleback brought her, or she herself could
easily catch, and also on the little stores that
she had buried at other times.   She knew every
Prairie-dog town in the region, as well as all the
best places for Mice and Rabbits.

Not far from the den was the very Dog-town
that first she had crossed the day she had gained
her liberty and lost her tail.   If she were capa-
ble of such retrospect, she must have laughed
to herself to think what a fool she was then.

The change in her methods was now shown. Somewhat removed from the others, a Prairie-dog had made his den in the most approved style, and now when Tito peered over he was feeding on the grass ten yards from his own door. A Prairie-dog away from the others is, of course, easier to catch than one in the middle of the town, for he has but one pair of eyes to guard him; so Tito set about stalking this one. How was she to do it when there was no cover, nothing but short grass and a few low weeds? The Whitebear knows how to approach the Seal on the flat ice, and the Indian how to get within striking distance of the grazing Deer. Tito knew how to do the same trick, and although one of the town Owls flew over with a warning chuckle, Tito set about her plan. A Prairie-dog cannot see well unless he is sitting up on his hind legs; his eyes are of little use when he is nosing in the grass; and Tito knew this. Further, a yellowish-gray animal on a yellowish-gray landscape is invisible till it moves. Tito seemed to know that. So, without any attempt to crawl or hide, she walked gently up-wind toward the Prairie-dog. Up-

Fair Game.

wind, not in order to prevent the Prairie-dog
smelling her, but so that she could smell him,
which came to the same thing.  As soon as the
Prairie-dog sat up with some food in his hand
she froze into a statue.  As soon as he dropped
again to nose in the grass, she walked steadily
nearer, watching his every move so that she
might be motionless each time he sat up to see
what his distant brothers were barking at.  Once
or twice he seemed alarmed by the calls of his
friends, but he saw nothing and resumed his
feeding.  She soon cut the fifty yards down to
ten, and the ten to five, and still was undis-
covered.  Then, when again the Prairie-dog
dropped down to seek more fodder, she made a
quick dash, and bore him off kicking and squeal-
ing.  Thus does the angel of the pruning-knife
lop off those that are heedless and foolishly in-
different to the advantages of society.


## VII

TITO had many adventures in which she did not
come out so well.  Once she nearly caught an
Antelope fawn, but the hunt was spoiled by the

sudden appearance of the mother, who gave
Tito a stinging blow on the side of the head
and ended her hunt for that day. She never
again made that mistake—she had sense. Once
or twice she had to jump to escape the strike
of a Rattlesnake. Several times she had been
fired at by hunters with long-range rifles. And
more and more she had to look out for the terrible Gray Wolves. The Gray Wolf, of course,
is much larger and stronger than the Coyote,
but the Coyote has the advantage of speed,
and can always escape in the open. All it
must beware of is being caught in a corner.
Usually when a Gray Wolf howls the Coyotes
go quietly about their business elsewhere.

Tito had a curious fad, occasionally seen
among the Wolves and Coyotes, of carrying in
her mouth, for miles, such things as seemed to
be interesting and yet were not tempting as eat-
ables. Many a time had she trotted a mile or
two with an old Buffalo-horn or a cast-off shoe,
only to drop it when something else attracted
her attention. The cow-boys who remark these
things have various odd explanations to offer:
one, that it is done to stretch the jaws, or keep

them in practice, just as a man in training carries
weights.   Coyotes have, in common with Dogs
and Wolves, the habit of calling at certain
stations along their line of travel, to leave a
record of their visit.   These stations may be a
stone, a tree, a post, or an old Buffalo-skull, and
the Coyote calling there can learn, by the odor
and track of the last comer, just who the caller
was, whence he came, and whither he went.
The whole country is marked out by these in-
telligence depots.  •Now it often happens that
a Coyote that has not much else to do will carry
a dry bone or some other useless object in its
mouth, but sighting the signal-post, will go toward it to get the news, lay down the bone,
and afterward forget to take it along, so that
the signal-posts in time become further marked
with a curious collection of odds and ends.

This singular habit was the cause of a dis-
aster to the Chimney-pot Wolf-hounds, and a
corresponding advantage to the Coyotes in the
war.   Jake had laid a line of poison baits on
the western bluffs.   Tito knew what they were,
and spurned them as usual; but finding more
later, she gathered up three or four and crossed

the Little Missouri toward the ranch-house. This she circled at a safe distance; but when something made the pack of Dogs break out into clamor, Tito dropped the baits, and next day, when the Dogs were taken out for exercise, they found and devoured these scraps of meat, so that in ten minutes there were four hundred dollars' worth of Greyhounds lying dead. This led to an edict against poisoning in that district, and thus was a great boon to the Coyotes.

Tito quickly learned that not only each kind of game must be hunted in a special way, but different ones of each kind may require quite different treatment. The Prairie-dog with the outlying den was really an easy prey, but the town was quite compact now that he was gone. Near the centre of it was a fine, big, fat Prairie-dog, a perfect alderman, that she had made several vain attempts to capture. On one occasion she had crawled almost within leaping distance, when the angry *bizz* of a Rattlesnake just ahead warned her that she was in danger. Not that the Rattler cared anything about the Prairie-dog, but he did not wish to be disturbed; and Tito, who had an instinctive fear of the

# Tito

Snake, was forced to abandon the hunt. The open stalk proved an utter failure with the Alderman, for the situation of his den made every Dog in the town his sentinel; but he was too good to lose, and Tito waited until circumstances made a new plan.

All Coyotes have a trick of watching from a high lookout whatever passes along the roads. After it has passed they go down and examine its track. Tito had this habit, except that she was always careful to keep out of sight herself.

One day a wagon passed from the town to the southward. Tito lay low and watched it. Something dropped on the road. When the wagon was out of sight Tito sneaked down, first to smell the trail as a matter of habit, second to see what it was that had dropped. The object was really an apple, but Tito saw only an unattractive round green thing like a cactus-leaf without spines, and of a peculiar smell. She snuffed it, spurned it, and was about to pass on; but the sun shone on it so brightly, and it rolled so curiously when she pawed, that she picked it up in a mechanical way and trotted back over the rise, where she found herself at

the Dog-town. Just then two great Prairie-
hawks came skimming like pirates over the
plain. As soon as they were in sight the Prairie-
dogs all barked, jerking their tails at each bark,
and hid below. When all were gone Tito
walked on toward the hole of the big fat fellow
whose body she coveted, and dropping the
apple on the ground a couple of feet from the
rim of the crater that formed his home, she put
her nose down to enjoy the delicious smell of
Dog-fat. Even his den smelled more fragrant
than those of the rest. Then she went quietly
behind a greasewood-bush, in a lower place
some twenty yards away, and lay flat. After a
few seconds some venturesome Prairie-dog
looked out, and seeing nothing, gave the "all's
well" bark. One by one they came out, and
in twenty minutes the town was alive as before.
One of the last to come out was the fat old
Alderman. He always took good care of his
own precious self. He peered out cautiously a
few times, then climbed to the top of his
lookout. A Prairie-dog hole is shaped like a
funnel, going straight down. Around the top
of this is built a high ridge which serves as a

lookout, and also makes sure that, no matter
how they may slip in their hurry, they are certain to drop into the funnel and be swallowed
up by the all-protecting earth.   On the outside
the ground slopes away gently from the funnel.
Now, when the Alderman saw that strange
round thing at his threshold he was afraid.
Second inspection led him to believe that it
was not dangerous, but was probably interesting.
He went cautiously toward it, smelled it, and
tried to nibble it ; but the apple rolled away, for
it was round, and the ground was smooth as
well as sloping.   The Prairie-dog followed and
gave it a nip which satisfied him that the strange
object would make good eating.   But each time
he nibbled, it rolled farther away.   The coast
seemed clear, all the other Prairie-dogs were
out, so the fat Alderman did not hesitate to
follow up the dodging, shifting apple.

This way and that it wriggled, and he followed.   Of course it worked toward the low
place where grew the greasewood-bush.   The
little tastes of apple that he got only whetted
his appetite.   The Alderman was more and
more interested.   Foot by foot he was led from

his hole toward that old, familiar bush, and had no thought of anything but the joy of eating. And Tito curled herself and braced her sinewy legs, and measured the distance between, until it dwindled to not more than three good jumps; then up and like an arrow she went, and grabbed and bore him off at last.

Now it will never be known whether it was accident or design that led to the placing of that apple, but it proved important, and if such a thing were to happen once or twice to a smart Coyote,—and it is usually clever ones that get such chances,—it might easily grow into a new trick of hunting.

After a hearty meal Tito buried the rest in a cold place, not to get rid of it, but to hide it for future use; and a little later, when she was too weak to hunt much, her various hoards of this sort came in very useful. True, the meat had turned very strong; but Tito was not critical, and she had no fears or theories of microbes, so suffered no ill effects.

314

The Alderman and the Apple.

# Tito

## VIII

THE lovely Hiawathan spring was touching all things in the fairy Badlands. Oh, why are they called Badlands? If Nature sat down deliberately on the eighth day of creation and said, "Now work is done, let's play; let's make a place that shall combine everything that is finished and wonderful and beautiful— a paradise for man and bird and beast," it was surely then that she made these wild, fantastic hills, teeming with life, radiant with gayest flowers, varied with sylvan groves, bright with prairie sweeps and brimming lakes and streams. In foreground, offing, and distant hills that change at every step, we find some proof that Nature squandered here the riches that in other lands she used as sparingly as gold, with colorful sky above and colorful land below, and the distance blocked by sculptured buttes that are built of precious stones and ores, and tinged as by a lasting and unspeakable sunset. And yet, for all this ten times gorgeous wonderland enchanted, blind man has found no better name than one which says, *the road to it is hard.*

317

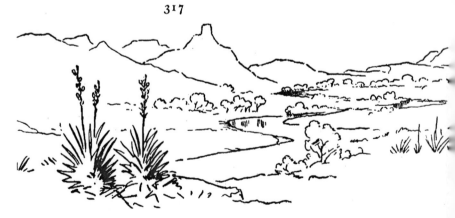

# Tito

The little hollow west of Chimney Butte was freshly grassed. The dangerous-looking Spanish bayonets, that through the bygone winter had waged war with all things, now sent out their contribution to the peaceful triumph of the spring, in flowers that have stirred even the chilly scientists to name them *Gloriosa ;* and the cactus, poisonous, most reptilian of herbs, surprised the world with a splendid bloom as little like itself as the pearl is like its mother shell-fish. The sage and the greasewood lent their gold, and the sand-anemone tinged the Badland hills like bluish snow ; and in the air and earth and hills on every hand was felt the fecund promise of the spring. This was the end of the winter famine, the beginning of the summer feast, and this was the time by the All-mother ordained when first the little Coyotes should see the light of day.

A mother does not have to learn to love her helpless, squirming brood. They bring the love with them—not much or little, not measurable, but perfect love. And in that dimly lighted warm abode she fondled them and licked them and cuddled them with heartful

318

warmth of tenderness that was as much a new epoch in her life as in theirs.

But the pleasure of loving them was measured in the same measure as anxiety for their safety. In bygone days her care had been mainly for herself. All she had learned in her strange puppyhood, all she had picked up since, was bent to the main idea of self-preservation. Now she was ousted from her own affections by her brood. Her chief care was to keep their home concealed, and this was not very hard at first, for she left them only when she must, to supply her own wants.

She came and went with great care, and only after spying well the land so that none should see and find the place of her treasure. If it were possible for the little ones' idea of their mother and the cow-boys' idea to be set side by side they would be found to have nothing in common, though both were right in their point of view. The ranchmen knew the Coyote only as a pair of despicable, cruel jaws, borne around on tireless legs, steered by incredible cunning, and leaving behind a track of destruction. The little ones knew her as a loving, gentle, all-

X

powerful guardian. For them her breast was soft and warm and infinitely tender. She fed and warmed them, she was their wise and watchful keeper. She was always at hand with food when they hungered, with wisdom to foil the cunning of their foes, and with a heart of courage tried to crown her well-laid plans for them with uniform success.

A baby Coyote is a shapeless, senseless, wriggling, and—to every one but its mother—a most uninteresting little lump. But after its eyes are open, after it has developed its legs, after it has learned to play in the sun with its brothers, or run at the gentle call of its mother when she brings home game for it to feed on, the baby Coyote becomes one of the cutest, dearest little rascals on earth. And when the nine that made up Coyotito's brood had reached this stage, it did not require the glamour of motherhood to make them objects of the greatest interest.

The summer was now on. The little ones were beginning to eat flesh-meat, and Tito, with some assistance from Saddleback, was kept busy to supply both themselves and the brood.

Tito and her Brood.

# Tito

Sometimes she brought them a Prairie-dog, at other times she would come home with a whole bunch of Gophers and Mice in her jaws; and once or twice, by the clever trick of relay-chasing, she succeeded in getting one of the big Northern Jack-rabbits for the little folks at home.

After they had feasted they would lie around in the sun for a time. Tito would mount guard on a bank and scan the earth and air with her keen, brassy eye, lest any dangerous foe should find their happy valley; and the merry pups played little games of tag, or chased the Butter-flies, or had apparently desperate encounters with each other, or tore and worried the bones and feathers that now lay about the threshold of the home. One, the least, for there is usu-ally a runt, stayed near the mother and climbed on her back or pulled at her tail. They made a lovely picture as they played, and the wrest-ling group in the middle seemed the focus of it all at first; but a keener, later look would have rested on the mother, quiet, watchful, not without anxiety, but, above all, with a face full of motherly tenderness. Oh, she was so proud

323

and happy, and she would sit there and watch them and silently love them till it was time to go home, or until some sign of distant danger showed. Then, with a low growl, she gave the signal, and all disappeared from sight in a twinkling, after which she would set off to meet and turn the danger, or go on a fresh hunt for food.

## IX

WOLVEK JAKE had several plans for making a fortune, but each in turn was abandoned as soon as he found that it meant work. At one time or other most men of this kind see the chance of their lives in a poultry-farm. They cherish the idea that somehow the poultry do all the work. And without troubling himself about the details, Jake devoted an unexpected windfall to the purchase of a dozen Turkeys for his latest scheme. The Turkeys were duly housed in one end of Jake's shanty, so as to be well guarded, and for a couple of days were the object of absorbing interest, and had the best of care—too much, really. But Jake's ardor waned about the third day; then the recurrent

324

necessity for long celebrations at Medora, and the ancient allurements of idle hours spent lying on the tops of sunny buttes and of days spent sponging on the hospitality of distant ranches, swept away the last pretence of attention to his poultry-farm. The Turkeys were utterly neglected—left to forage for themselves; and each time that Jake returned to his uninviting shanty, after a few days' absence, he found fewer birds, till at last none but the old Gobbler was left.

Jake cared little about the loss, but was filled with indignation against the thief.

He was now installed as wolver to the Broadarrow outfit. That is, he was supplied with poison, traps, and Horses, and was also entitled to all he could make out of Wolf bounties. A reliable man would have gotten pay in addition, for the ranchmen are generous, but Jake was not reliable.

Every wolver knows, of course, that his business naturally drops into several well-marked periods.

In the late winter and early spring—the love-season—the Hounds will not hunt a She-wolf. They will quit the trail of a He-wolf at this time

to take up that of a She-wolf, but when they do overtake her, they, for some sentimental reason, invariably let her go in peace. In August and September the young Coyotes and Wolves are just beginning to run alone, and they are then easily trapped and poisoned. A month or so later the survivors have learned how to take care of themselves, but in the early summer the wolver knows that there are dens full of little ones all through the hills. Each den has from five to fifteen pups, and the only difficulty is to know the whereabouts of these family homes.

One way of finding the dens is to watch from some tall butte for a Coyote carrying food to its brood. As this kind of wolving involved much lying still, it suited Jake very well. So, equipped with a Broad-arrow Horse and the boss's field-glasses, he put in week after week at den-hunting—that is, lying asleep in some possible lookout, with an occasional glance over the country when it seemed easier to do that than to lie still.

The Coyotes had learned to avoid the open. They generally went homeward along the sheltered hollows; but this was not always possible,

and one day, while exercising his arduous pro-
fession in the country west of Chimney Butte,
Jake's glasses and glance fell by chance on a
dark spot which moved along an open hillside.
It was gray, and it looked like this: and even
Jake knew that that meant Coyote. If it had
been a gray Wolf it would have been so: with
tail up. A Fox would have looked so: the
large ears and tail and the yellow color would
have marked it. And a Deer would have looked
so: That dark shade from the front end meant
something in his mouth,—probably something
being carried home,—and that would mean a
den of little ones.

He made careful note of the place, and returned there next day to watch, selecting a high
butte near where he had seen the Coyote carrying the food. But all day passed, and he saw
nothing. Next day, however, he descried a
dark Coyote, old Saddleback, carrying a large
Bird, and by the help of the glasses he made
out that it was a Turkey, and then he knew that
the yard at home was quite empty, and he also
knew where the rest of them had gone, and
vowed terrible vengeance when he should find

the den. He followed Saddleback with his
eyes as far as possible, and that was no great
way, then went to the place to see if he could
track him any farther; but he found no guiding
signs, and he did not chance on the little hollow
that was the playground of Tito's brood.

Meanwhile Saddleback came to the little
hollow and gave the low call that always con-
jured from the earth the unruly procession of
the nine riotous little pups, and they dashed at
the Turkey and pulled and worried till it was
torn up, and each that got a piece ran to one
side alone and silently proceeded to eat, seizing
his portion in his jaws when another came near,
and growling his tiny growl as he showed the
brownish whites of his eyes in his effort to
watch the intruder. Those that got the softer
parts to feed on were well fed. But the three
that did not turned all their energies on the
frame of the Gobbler, and over that there waged
a battle royal. This way and that they tugged
and tussled, getting off occasional scraps, but
really hindering each other feeding, till Tito
glided in and deftly cut the Turkey into three
or four, when each dashed off with a prize, over

which he sat and chewed and smacked his lips
and jammed his head down sideways to bring
the backmost teeth to bear, while the baby runt
scrambled into the home den, carrying in triumph his share—the Gobbler's grotesque head
and neck.

## X

JAKE felt that he had been grievously wronged,
indeed ruined, by that Coyote that stole his
Turkeys.  He vowed he would skin them alive
when he found the pups, and took pleasure in
thinking about how he would do it.  His attempt to follow Saddleback by trailing was a
failure, and all his searching for the den was
useless, but he had come prepared for any
emergency.  In case he found the den he had
brought a pick and shovel; in case he did not
he had brought a living white Hen.

The Hen he now took to a broad open place
near where he had seen Saddleback, and there
he tethered her to a stick of wood that she
could barely drag.  Then he made himself comfortable on a lookout that was near, and lay still
to watch.  The Hen, of course, ran to the end

of the string, and then lay on the ground flop-
ping stupidly. Presently the clog gave enough
to ease the strain, she turned by mere chance
in another direction, and so, for a time, stood
up to look around.

The day went slowly by, and Jake lazily
stretched himself on the blanket in his spying-
place. Toward evening Tito came by on a
hunt. This was not surprising, for the den was
only half a mile away. Tito had learned, among
other rules, this, " Never show yourself on the
sky-line." In former days the Coyotes used to
trot along the tops of the ridges for the sake of
the chance to watch both sides. But men and
guns had taught Tito that in this way you are
sure to be seen. She therefore made a practice
of running along near the top, and once in a
while peeping over.

This was what she did that evening as she
went out to hunt for the children's supper, and
her keen eyes fell on the white Hen, stupidly
stalking about and turning up its eyes in a wise
way each time a harmless Turkey-buzzard came
in sight against a huge white cloud.

Tito was puzzled. This was something new.

It *looked* like game, but she feared to take
any chances. She circled all around without
showing herself, then decided that, whatever it
might be, it was better let alone. As she passed
on, a faint whiff of smoke caught her attention.
She followed cautiously, and under a butte far
from the Hen she found Jake's camp. His bed
was there, his Horse was picketed, and on the
remains of the fire was a pot which gave out a
smell which she well knew about men's camps
—the smell of coffee. Tito felt uneasy at this
proof that a man was staying so near her home,
but she went off quietly on her hunt, keeping
out of sight, and Jake knew nothing of her
visit.

About sundown he took in his decoy Hen, as
Owls were abundant, and went back to his
camp.

## XI

NEXT day the Hen was again put out, and late
that afternoon Saddleback came trotting by.
As soon as his eye fell on the white Hen he
stopped short, his head on one side, and gazed.
Then he circled to get the wind, and went cau-

tiously sneaking nearer, very cautiously, somewhat puzzled, till he got a whiff that reminded him of the place where he had found those Turkeys. The Hen took alarm, and tried to run away; but Saddleback made a rush, seized the Hen so fiercely that the string was broken, and away he dashed toward the home valley.

Jake had fallen asleep, but the squawk of the Hen happened to awaken him, and he sat up in time to see her borne away in old Saddleback's jaws.

As soon as they were out of sight Jake took up the white-feather trail. At first it was easily followed, for the Hen had shed plenty of plumes in her struggles; but once she was dead in Saddleback's jaws, very few feathers were dropped except where she was carried through the brush. But Jake was following quietly and certainly, for Saddleback had gone nearly in a straight line home to the little ones with the dangerous telltale prize. Once or twice there was a puzzling delay when the Coyote had changed his course or gone over an open place; but one white feather was good for fifty yards, and when the daylight was gone, Jake was not two hun-

dred yards from the hollow, in which at that
very moment were the nine little pups, having
a perfectly delightful time with the Hen, pulling it to pieces, feasting and growling, sneezing
the white feathers from their noses or coughing
them from their throats.

If a puff of wind had now blown from them
toward Jake, it might have carried a flurry of
snowy plumes or even the merry cries of the
little revellers, and the den would have been
discovered at once.  But, as luck would have
it, the evening lull was on, and all distant sounds
were hidden by the crashing that Jake made in
trying to trace his feather guides through the
last thicket.

About this time Tito was returning home
with a Magpie that she had captured by watching till it went to feed within the ribs of a
dead Horse, when she ran across Jake's trail.
Now, a man on foot is always a suspicious character in this country.  She followed the trail for
a little to see where he was going, and that she
knew at once from the scent.  How it tells her
no one can say, yet all hunters know that it does.
And Tito marked that it was going straight

333

toward her home. Thrilled with new fear, she hid the Bird she was carrying, then followed the trail of the man. Within a few minutes she could hear him in the thicket, and Tito realized the terrible danger that was threatening. She went swiftly, quietly around to the den hollow, came on the heedless little roisterers, after giving the signal-call, which prevented them taking alarm at her approach; but she must have had a shock when she saw how marked the hollow and the den were now, all drifted over with feathers white as snow. Then she gave the danger-call that sent them all to earth, and the little glade was still.

Her own nose was so thoroughly and always her guide that it was not likely she thought of the white feathers being the telltale. But now she realized that a man, one she knew of old as a treacherous character, one whose scent had always meant mischief to her, that had been associated with all her own troubles and the cause of nearly all her desperate danger, was close to her darlings; was tracking them down; in a few minutes would surely have them in his merciless power.

334

Oh, the wrench to the mother's heart at the thought of what she could foresee! But the warmth of the mother-love lent life to the mother-wit. Having sent the little ones out of sight, and by a sign conveyed to Saddleback her alarm, she swiftly came back to the man, then she crossed before him, thinking, in her half-reasoning way, that the man *must* be following a foot-scent just as she herself would do, but would, of course, take the stronger line of tracks she was now laying. She did not realize that the failing daylight made any difference. Then she trotted to one side, and to make doubly sure of being followed, she uttered the fiercest challenge she could, just as many a time she had done to make the Dogs pursue her:

Grrr-wow-wow-wa-a-a-h,

and stood still; then ran a little nearer and did it again, and then again much nearer, and repeated her bark, she was so determined that the wolver should follow her.

Of course the wolver could see nothing of the Coyote, for the shades were falling. He

335

Y

had to give up the hunt anyway. His understanding of the details was as different as possible from that the Mother Coyote had, and
yet it came to the same thing. He recognized
that the Coyote's bark was the voice of the distressed mother trying to call him away. So he
knew the brood must be close at hand, and all
he now had to do was return in the morning and
complete his search. So he made his way back
to his camp.

## XII

SADDLEBACK thought they had won the victory.
He felt secure, because the foot-scent that he
might have supposed the man to be following
would be stale by morning. Tito did not feel
so safe. That two-legged beast was close to
her home and her little ones; had barely been
turned aside; might come back yet.

The wolver watered and repicketed his Horse,
kindled the fire anew, made his coffee and ate
his evening meal, then smoked awhile before
lying down to sleep, thinking occasionally of
the little woolly scalps he expected to gather in
the morning.

336

He was about to roll up in his blanket when, out of the dark distance, there sounded the evening cry of the Coyote, the rolling challenge of more than one voice. Jake grinned in fiendish glee, and said: "There you are all right. Howl some more. I'll see you in the morning."

It was the ordinary, or rather *one* of the ordinary, camp-calls of the Coyote. It was sounded once, and then all was still. Jake soon forgot it in his loggish slumber.

The callers were Tito and Saddleback. The challenge was not an empty bluff. It had a distinct purpose behind it—to know for sure whether the enemy had any dogs with him; and because there was no responsive bark Tito knew that he had none.

Then Tito waited for an hour or so till the flickering fire had gone dead, and the only sound of life about the camp was the cropping of the grass by the picketed Horse. Tito crept near softly, so softly that the Horse did not see her till she was within twenty feet; then he gave a start that swung the tightened picket-rope up into the air, and snorted gently. Tito went quietly forward, and opening her wide gape, took the rope in, almost under her ears, between the great scissor-like back teeth, then chewed it for a few seconds. The fibres quickly frayed, and, aided by the strain the nervous Horse still kept up, the last of the strands gave way, and the Horse was free. He was not much alarmed ; he knew the smell of Coyote ; and after jumping three steps and walking six, he stopped.

The sounding thumps of his hoofs on the ground awoke the sleeper. He looked up, but, seeing the Horse standing there, he went calmly off to sleep again, supposing that all went well.

Tito had sneaked away, but she now returned like a shadow, avoided the sleeper, but came around, sniffed doubtfully at the coffee, and then puzzled over a tin can, while Saddleback examined the frying-pan full of " camp-sinkers " and then defiled both cakes and pan with dirt. The bridle hung on a low bush ; the Coyotes did not know what it was, but just for luck they cut it into several pieces, then, taking the sacks that held Jake's bacon and flour, they carried them far away and buried them in the sand.

# Tito

Having done all the mischief she could, Tito, followed by her mate, now set off for a wooded gully some miles away, where was a hole that had been made first by a Chipmunk, but enlarged by several other animals, including a Fox that had tried to dig out its occupants. Tito stopped and looked at many possible places before she settled on this. Then she set to work to dig. Saddleback had followed in a half-comprehending way, till he saw what she was doing. Then when she, tired with digging, came out, he went into the hole, and after snuffing about went on with the work, throwing out the earth between his hind legs; and when it was piled up behind he would come out and push it yet farther away.

And so they worked for hours, not a word said, and yet with a sufficient comprehension of the object in view to work in relief of each other. And by the time the morning came they had a den big enough to do for their home, in case they must move, though it would not compare with the one in the grassy hollow.

339

## XIII

I⊤ was nearly sunrise before the wolver awoke.
With the true instinct of a plainsman he turned
to look for the Horse. *It was gone.* What his
ship is to the sailor, what wings are to the Bird,
what money is to the merchant, the Horse is to
the plainsman. Without it he is helpless, lost
at sea, wing broken, crippled in business.
Afoot on the plains is the sum of earthly terrors. Even Jake realized this, and ere his
foggy wits had fully felt the shock he sighted
the steed afar on a flat, grazing and stepping
ever farther from the camp. At a second
glance Jake noticed that the Horse was trailing
the rope. If the rope had been left behind
Jake would have known that it was hopeless to
try to catch him; he would have finished his
den-hunt and found the little Coyotes. But,
with the trailing rope, there was a good chance
of catching the Horse; so Jake set out to try.

Of all maddening things there is nothing
worse than to be almost, but not quite, able to
catch your Horse. Do what he might, Jake
could not get quite near enough to seize that

short rope, and the Horse led him on and on, until at last they were well on the homeward trail.

Now Jake was afoot anyhow, so seeing no better plan, he set out to follow that Horse right back to the Ranch.

But when about seven miles were covered Jake succeeded in catching him. He rigged up a rough *jáquima* with the rope and rode barebacked in fifteen minutes over the three miles that lay between him and the Sheep-ranch, giving vent all the way to his pent-up feelings in cruel abuse of that Horse. Of course it did not do any good, and he knew that, but he considered it was heaps of satisfaction.

Here Jake got a meal and borrowed a saddle and a mongrel Hound that could run a trail, and returned late in the afternoon to finish his den-hunt. Had he known it, he now could have found it without the aid of the cur, for it was really close at hand when he took up the feather-trail where last he had left it. Within one hundred yards he rose to the top of the little ridge; then just over it, almost face to face, he came on a Coyote, carrying in its

341

mouth a large Rabbit.   The Coyote leaped just
at the same moment that Jake fired his revolver,
and the Dog broke into a fierce yelling and
dashed off in pursuit, while Jake blazed and
blazed away, without effect, and wondered why
the Coyote should still hang on to that Rabbit
as she ran for her life with the Dog yelling at
her heels.   Jake followed as far as he could
and fired at each chance, but scored no hit.
So when they had vanished among the buttes
he left the Dog to follow or come back as he
pleased, while he returned to the den, which, of
course, was plain enough now.   Jake knew that
the pups were there yet.   Had he not seen the
mother bringing a Rabbit for them?

So he set to work with pick and shovel all
the rest of that day.   There were plenty of
signs that the den had inhabitants, and, duly
encouraged, he dug on, and after several hours
of the hardest work he had ever done, he came
to the end of the den—*only to find it empty.*
After cursing his luck at the first shock of dis-
gust, he put on his strong leather glove and
groped about in the nest.   He felt something
firm and drew it out.   It was the head and

## Tito

neck of his own Turkey Gobbler, and that was
all he got for his pains.

## XIV

Tito had not been idle during the time that
the enemy was Horse-hunting. Whatever Saddleback might have done, Tito would live in no
fool's paradise. Having finished the new den,
she trotted back to the little valley of feathers,
and the first young one that came to meet her
at the door of this home was a broad-headed
one much like herself. She seized him by the
neck and set off, carrying him across country
toward the new den, a couple of miles away.
Every little while she had to put her offspring
down to rest and give it a chance to breathe.
This made the moving slow, and the labor of
transporting the pups occupied all that day, for
Saddleback was not allowed to carry any of
them, probably because he was too rough.

Beginning with the biggest and brightest,
they were carried away one at a time, and late
in the afternoon only the runt was left. Tito
had not only worked at digging all night, she

343

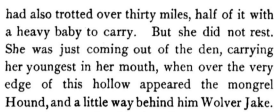

had also trotted over thirty miles, half of it with a heavy baby to carry. But she did not rest. She was just coming out of the den, carrying her youngest in her mouth, when over the very edge of this hollow appeared the mongrel Hound, and a little way behind him Wolver Jake.

Away went Tito, holding the baby tight, and away went the Dog behind her.

*Bang! bang! bang!* said the revolver.

But not a shot touched her. Then over the ridge they dashed, where the revolver could not reach her, and sped across a flat, the tired Coyote and her baby, and the big fierce Hound behind her, bounding his hardest. Had she been fresh and unweighted she could soon have left the clumsy cur that now was barking furiously on her track and rather gaining than losing in the race. But she put forth all her strength, careered along a slope, where she gained a little, then down across a brushy flat where the cruel bushes robbed her of all she had gained. But again into the open they came, and the wolver, laboring far behind, got sight of them and fired again and again with his revolver, and only stirred the dust, but still

344

Tito's Race for Life.

it made her dodge and lose time, and it also
spurred the Dog. The hunter saw the Coyote,
his old acquaintance of the bobtail, carrying
still, as he thought, the Jack-rabbit she had been
bringing to her brood, and wondered at her
strange persistence. "Why doesn't she drop
that weight when flying for her life?" But on
she went and gamely bore her load over the
hills, the man cursing his luck that he had not
brought his Horse, and the mongrel bounding in
deadly earnest but thirty feet behind her.
Then suddenly in front of Tito yawned a little
cut-bank gully. Tired and weighted, she dared
not try the leap; she skirted around. But the
Dog was fresh; he cleared it easily, and the
mother's start was cut down by half. But on she
went, straining to hold the little one high above
the scratching brush and the dangerous bay-
onet-spikes; but straining too much, for the
helpless cub was choking in his mother's grip.
She must lay him down or strangle him; with
such a weight she could not much longer keep
out of reach. She tried to give the howl for
help, but her voice was muffled by the cub,
now struggling for breath, and as she tried to

ease her grip on him a sudden wrench jerked him from her mouth into the grass—into the power of the merciless Hound. Tito was far smaller than the Dog; ordinarily she would have held him in fear; but her little one, her baby, was the only thought now, and as the brute sprang forward to tear it in his wicked jaws, she leaped between and stood facing him with all her mane erect, her teeth exposed, and plainly showed her resolve to save her young one at any price. The Dog was not brave, only confident that he was bigger and had the man behind him. But the man was far away, and balked in his first rush at the trembling little Coyote, that tried to hide in the grass, the cur hesitated a moment, and Tito howled the long howl for help—the muster-call:

Yap-yap-yap-yah-yah-yah-h-h-h-h
Yap-yap-yap-yah-yah-yah-h-h-h-h,

and made the buttes around reëcho so that Jake could not tell where it came from; but some one else there was that heard and did know whence it came. The Dog's courage revived on hearing something like a far-away

348

shout. Again he sprang at the little one, but again the mother balked him with her own body, and then they closed in deadly struggle. "Oh, if Saddleback would only come!" But no one came, and now she had no further chance to call. Weight is everything in a closing fight, and Tito soon went down, bravely fighting to the last, but clearly worsted; and the Hound's courage grew with the sight of victory, and all he thought of now was to finish her and then kill her helpless baby in its turn. He had no ears or eyes for any other thing, till out of the nearest sage there flashed a streak of gray, and in a trice the big-voiced coward was hurled back by a foe almost as heavy as himself— hurled back with a crippled shoulder. Dash, chop, and stanch old Saddleback sprang on him again. Tito struggled to her feet, and they closed on him together. His courage fled at once when he saw the odds, and all he wanted now was safe escape—escape from Saddleback, whose speed was like the wind, escape from Tito, whose baby's life was at stake. Not twenty jumps away did he get; not breath enough had he to howl for help to his master in the distant

349

hills; not fifteen yards away from her little one
that he meant to tear, they tore him all to bits.

And Tito lifted the rescued young one, and
travelling as slowly as she wished, they reached
the new-made den. There the family safely
reunited, far away from danger of further attack by Wolver Jake or his kind.

And there they lived in peace till their mother
had finished their training, and every one of
them grew up wise in the ancient learning of
the plains, wise in the later wisdom that the
ranchers' war has forced upon them, and not
only they, but their children's children, too.

THE Buffalo herds have gone; they have suc-
cumbed to the rifles of the hunters. The Antelope droves are nearly gone; Hound and lead
were too much for them. The Blacktail bands
have dwindled before axe and fence. The
ancient dwellers of the Badlands have faded
like snow under the new conditions, but the
Coyotes are no more in fear of extinction.
Their morning and evening song still sounds
from the level buttes, as it did long years ago
when every plain was a teeming land of game.

They have learned the deadly secrets of traps
and poisons, they know how to baffle the
gunner and Hound, they have matched their
wits with the hunter's wits.   They have learned
how to prosper in a land of man-made plenty,
in spite of the worst that man can do, and it
was Tito that taught them how.

z

# Why the Chickadee Goes Crazy
# Once a Year

Published September, 1893, in "Our Animal Friends,"
the organ of the American Society for the Prevention of
Cruelty to Animals

# Why the Chickadee Goes Crazy Once a Year

LONG time ago, when there was no winter in the north, the Chickadees lived merrily in the woods with their relatives, and cared for nothing but to get all the pleasure possible out of their daily life in the thickets. But at length Mother Carey sent them all a warning that they must move to the south, for hard frost and snow were coming on their domains, with starvation close behind.

The Nuthatches and other cousins of the Chickadees took this warning seriously, and set about learning how and when to go; but Tomtit, who led his brothers, only laughed and

355

# Why the Chickadee Goes Crazy

turned a dozen wheels around a twig that served him for a trapeze.

"Go to the south?" said he. "Not I; I am too well contented here; and as for frost and snow, I never saw any and have no faith in them."

But the Nuthatches and Kinglets were in such a state of bustle that at length the Chickadees did catch a little of the excitement, and left off play for a while to question their friends; and they were not pleased with what they learned, for it seemed that all of them were to make a journey that would last many days, and the little Kinglets were actually going as far as the Gulf of Mexico. Besides, they were to fly by night in order to avoid their enemies the Hawks, and the weather at this season was sure to be stormy. So the Chickadees said it was all nonsense, and went off in a band, singing and chasing one another through the woods.

But their cousins were in earnest. They bustled about making their preparations, and learned beforehand what it was necessary for them to know about the way. The great wide river running southward, the moon at height,

## Why the Chickadee Goes Crazy

and the trumpeting of the Geese were to be their guides, and they were to sing as they flew in the darkness, to keep from being scattered.

The noisy, rollicking Chickadees were noisier than ever as the preparations went on, and made sport of their relatives, who were now gathered in great numbers in the woods along the river; and at length, when the proper time of the moon came, the cousins arose in a body and flew away in the gloom. The Chickadees said that the cousins all were crazy, made some good jokes about the Gulf of Mexico, and then dashed away in a game of tag through the woods, which, by the by, seemed rather deserted now, while the weather, too, was certainly turning remarkably cool.

At length the frost and snow really did come, and the Chickadees were in a woful case. Indeed, they were frightened out of their wits, and dashed hither and thither, seeking in vain for some one to set them aright on the way to the south. They flew wildly about the woods. till they were truly crazy. I suppose there was not a Squirrel-hole or a hollow log in the neighborhood that some Chickadee did not enter to

357

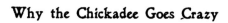

## Why the Chickadee Goes Crazy

inquire if this was the Gulf of Mexico. But no one could tell anything about it, no one was going that way, and the great river was hidden under ice and snow.

About this time a messenger from Mother Carey was passing with a message to the Caribou in the far north; but all he could tell the Chickadees was that *he* could not be their guide, as he had no instructions, and, at any rate, he was going the other way. Besides, he told them they had had the same notice as their cousins whom they had called "crazy"; and from what he knew of Mother Carey, they would probably have to brave it out here all through the snow, not only now, but in all following winters; so they might as well make the best of it.

This was sad news for the Tomtits; but they were brave little fellows, and seeing they could not help themselves, they set about making the best of it. Before a week had gone by they were in their usual good spirits again, scrambling about the twigs or chasing one another as before. They had still the assurance that winter would end. So filled were they with this

358

# Why the Chickadee Goes Crazy

idea that even at its commencement, when a fresh blizzard came on, they would gleefully remark to one another that it was a "sign of spring," and one or another of the band would lift his voice in the sweet little chant that we all know so well:

*Spring soon*

another would take it up and reëcho:

*Spring com-ing*

and they would answer and repeat the song until the dreary woods rang again with the good news, and people learned to love the brave little Bird that sets his face so cheerfully to meet so hard a case.

But to this day, when the chill wind blows through the deserted woods, the Chickadees seem to lose their wits for a few days, and dart into all sorts of odd and dangerous places. They may then be found in great cities, or open prairies, cellars, chimneys, and hollow logs; and the next time you find one of the wanderers in any such place, be sure to remember that Tomtit goes crazy once a year, and probably went into his strange retreat in search of the Gulf of Mexico.

THE THOUGHT

CPSIA information can be obtained at www.ICGtesting.com
Printed in the USA
LVOW11s1750151215

466719LV00001B/66/P

9 781443 702980